Weighing up the Evidence

HOW AND WHY:

The Second World War

Sarah Harris

Dryad Press, London

Contents

ISBN 0 85219 805 1

First published 198[illegible]
Typeset by Tek-Art Ltd, Kent
and printed in Great Britain by The Bath Pre[illegible]
for the Publishers, Dryad Press
4 Fitzhardinge Street, London W1H 0AH

Introduction

To the British and the Americans the Second World War is a popular war, full of heroic stories. It was fought on sound moral issues; a clean war, a just war, an "ideologically sound" war. The evils of Nazism, confirmed at the liberation of the death camps, and the wickedness of the Japanese, confirmed at the sight of Allied soldiers starved and beaten in the prisoner-of-war camps, offered proof, if proof were needed, that here was a war to be proud of. Here was a crusade: no need to agonize over whether the British dead had sacrificed their lives in vain; no need to hide away the veterans and pretend that none of it ever happened.

This view of the Second World War as heroic and just has coloured popular perception of how and by whom the war was caused. People have blamed the failure of Britain's leaders to stand up to Hitler in the first years of his territorial expansion. They have condemned the policy of appeasement, which the French and British governments chose to follow, as a policy of weakness which exacerbated Hitler's aggressive instincts and directly caused the difficult war that followed. "Appeasement" has become a dirty word in politics.

People have also seen the American policy of isolationism – refusing to become involved in European affairs after 1919 – as having contributed to the disaster that befell Europe. Without America, Britain and France were not strong enough to stand against Germany. By failing to live up to her responsibilities, the argument goes, America created the situation in which, once again, thousands of her young men had to die on foreign soil.

These views, held by many and based on the first historical interpretations of the war, have coloured our political behaviour as nations on many subsequent occasions. In the Suez Crisis, the invasion of Egypt by British troops was justified partly by likening the Egyptian Nationalist leader, Nasser, to Hitler. This likeness, it was argued, "proved" that Nasser's demands to nationalize the Suez Canal should not be conceded. When British troops were sent to the Falkland Islands, one of the arguments used to support the war against Argentina was that people's rights to self-determination and freedom from dictators should be upheld. The fate of the Czech people at the hands of Hitler and the Western leaders was not far from people's thoughts. American policy in South East Asia, which led to the involvement of US armies in difficult wars in Korea and Vietnam, was based on the observation of the fate of small European nations at the hands of Hitler. Although this time the Soviet Union was seen as the aggressor, the principles were held to be the same. The fear of America returning to the isolation of the 1930s, which many feel contributed to Hitler's success, is a powerful motivator in European defence policy, where preserving American involvement in Europe often outweighs other defence priorities.

When politicians have used interpretations of the past to defend policies which might otherwise be unpopular, it becomes important to them and to their supporters that those interpretations remain accepted as the truth. Each generation of historians, however, seeks to write its own account of the past. As more and more sources become available for study, and as societies change and develop, new ideas are aired and new interpretations are offered for old events.

In the last twenty years, historians have increasingly offered evidence to suggest that the policy of appeasement was not morally bankrupt: that to condemn the British and French leaders for their policies is to judge with the benefit of hindsight. Some argue that you cannot leave out the determination of Hitler for an aggressive outcome, whatever the Allies did or did not do.

New evidence also about the war in the Far East has been explored, and historians have put forward new ideas from which to develop an understanding of the causes of the war and the motives of the Japanese government of the 1930s.

This book explores some of these ideas, old and new. It brings together contemporary accounts from both official government papers and more personal observations. It looks at cartoons and other visual evidence, and studies figures and points of view, in the hope that you will be able to develop your own opinions as to where the causes of the Second World War may be found. The question is a difficult one, for there are many threads to trace through complicated patterns before answers begin to make sense.

The book starts by presenting a series of popular images of the war, so that the event itself that we are endeavouring to explain is clear in our minds. While we can never banish outcomes from our thinking (after all, it is because of the outcomes that we are exploring the events in the first place), it is well to remind ourselves that those outcomes themselves bias our judgments about the causes.

The next section, "Filling in the Background", looks in a broad way at the problems and ideas that were at play in the world between the end of the First World War and 1937, which most historians regard as a turning point on the road to war in both East and West. A closer and more detailed investigation of Europe, America and the Far East between 1937 and the commencement of world war in 1941 is then undertaken. Finally there is a brief reminder of the consequences of all these events.

On pages 59-63 you will find a date list, a glossary to help you with the particular meaning of any words which you may not understand, an analysis of the types of sources of evidence we use, their usefulness and reliability, and a series of biographies of those "guilty men" and "aggressors" who made the history we study.

Images of the Second World War

Often our images of the Second World War are confused and confusing. It is a war which people remember as being, or which we have been told was clear-cut in its issues. Germany and Japan were baddies, Italy was silly, France was incompetent, and Britain and America were goodies. It is a war of dashing heroes such as Guy Gibson and his Dambusters, or Douglas Bader in the Battle of Britain, and of virtuous heroines like Odette Churchill and Violette Szabo. Television provides images of the war: pictures of humour in *'Allo 'Allo* and the Cafe Renée, of stoicism in *Colditz*, of deprivation and death in *Tenko*. Other images of the war are those of Auschwitz and Belsen, gas chambers and mass murder, atomic war and death and destruction in Hiroshima and Nagasaki. The Second World War is also the war that killed some of your grandparents and their friends.

BRITAIN STOOD ALONE

Winston Churchill, 10 May 1940:

I would say to the House as I have said to those who have joined this Government: 'I have nothing to offer but blood, toil, tears and sweat'. We have before us an ordeal of the most grievous kind.

We have before us many, many long months of struggle and of suffering. You ask: 'What is our policy?' I will say: 'It is to wage war by sea, land, and air, with all our might, and with all the strength that God can give us; to wage war against a monstrous tyranny, never surpassed in the dark lamentable catalogue of human crime'. That is our policy. You ask: 'What is our aim?' I can answer in one word: 'Victory!' Victory at all costs, victory in spite of all terror, victory, however long and hard the road may be, for without victory there is no survival!

(*Source:* W.S. Churchill, Prime Minister, 10 May 1940)

Who or what was the "monstrous tyranny"?

WAR FOUGHT IN THE AIR

German bombers:

The first flight of German bombers was coming . . . to start the twelve hour attack against London. . . . The Hurricanes and Spitfires were already in the air . . . the German bombers, flying in V-formation, began pouring in. . .

The Germans were sending in two or three planes at a time, sometimes only one, in relays. They would pass overhead. The guns and lights would follow them, and in about five minutes we could hear the hollow grunt of the bombs. Huge pear-shaped bursts of flame would rise up into the smoke and disappear. The world was upside-down. . .

It was like a shuttle service, the way the German planes came up the Thames, the fires acting as a flare path. Often they were above the smoke. The searchlights bored into that black roof but couldn't penetrate it.

They looked like long pillars supporting a black canopy. Suddenly all the lights dashed off, and a blackness fell right to the ground. It grew cold. We covered ourselves with hay. The shrapnel clicked as it kicked the concrete road nearby, and still the German bombers came.

(*Source:* Ed Murrow broadcasting on the Battle of Britain, 1940, quoted in Duffy, *The Twentieth Century*, Blackwell, 1983)

British bombers:

You may ask how we, who know what heavy bombing means, feel about this appalling and devastating raid on Cologne... We are ... sorry for the women and children who may have suffered for the stupidity of their menfolk in putting Hitler in power and their cowardice in keeping him there. We are sorry for them, but when we remember Warsaw, Rotterdam, Coventry and Belgrade ... we harden our hearts ... if the helpless populations of the occupied lands, from Russia to France are to have their terrible ordeal curtailed – then such things as happened in Cologne last night must happen elsewhere in Germany again and again ... to teach the German people so that they will never forget it, the truth of the warning: 'He who lives by the sword shall perish by the sword.'

(*Source:* BBC broadcast to Occupied Europe, 1 June 1944, quoted in Duffy, *The Twentieth Century*, Blackwell, 1983)

Do you think this is a good justification for bombing raids?

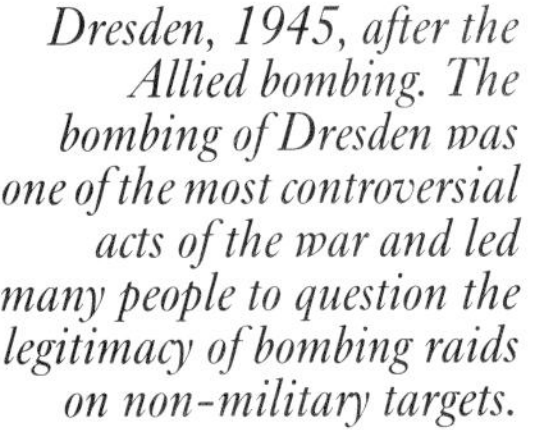

Dresden, 1945, after the Allied bombing. The bombing of Dresden was one of the most controversial acts of the war and led many people to question the legitimacy of bombing raids on non-military targets.

TANKS

Tanks were used to great military effect by the German army in its *Blitzkrieg* tactics, which brought the Germans so many victories in the first years of the war. They were not always comfortable companions:

A tank you see, had four petrol tanks and each one was filled with high octane. If any of these four were hit the whole lot would go up. . . . Now there were two ways to get out. One was via the turret; the other was through a trap door on the opposite side of the driver. . . . Often the turret would be inaccessible . . . ; if the machine was hit badly the trap door would jam as well . . . if both the turret and the trap door were jammed . . . you'd die! It takes twenty minutes for a medium tank to incinerate; and the flames burn slowly, so figure it takes ten minutes for a hearty man within to perish. You wouldn't even be able to struggle, for chances are both exits would be sheeted with flame and smoke. You would sit, read *Good Housekeeping*, and die like a dog.

(*Source:* Neil Frankel, *Patton's Best*)

Tanks moving forward at El Alamein, North Africa, October 1942.

Good News

for growing

children

A small quantity of Cadburys Milk Chocolate has been made. All the food value of full-cream milk is retained in this chocolate. For growing children who need the extra nourishment, it is a rare wartime treat.
The amount is small but it is being distributed fairly in the areas we supply. When your turn comes, please see that the children get it.

CADBURYS
Milk
Chocolate

UTILITY
CASH PRICES
Divan 6' x 2' 6" - - - £5.13.6
Dressing Chest 3' wide £9.15.0
Wardrobe 4' wide - - £15.16.6
or - ON OUR
EASY TERMS
The Times
FURNISHING COMPANY
235-238 HIGH HOLBORN, W.C.1. Branches all over England

Advertisements from Picture Post, *12 August 1944. Why might an historian regard the Cadbury's advertisement as particularly reliable evidence of shortages?*

WOMEN CALLED TO THE FRONT LINE

Citation on the award of military medals to two WAAF telephonists stationed at Biggin Hill:

When enemy bombers heavily attacked an RAF Fighter Command Station in September 1940, Cpl Henderson and Sgt Turner were on duty in a building which received a direct hit. Sgt Turner was the switchboard operator and Cpl Henderson was in charge of a special telephone line.

Bombs were falling around the building, but both women carried on with their jobs although they knew there was only a light roof over their heads. When the building received a direct hit both continued working till it caught fire and they were ordered to leave.

(*Source:* quoted in Katherine Beauman, *Wings on Her Shoulders*, Hutchinson, 1944)

The Hand that held the Hoover drives the Van!
HOUSEWIFE 1944
With all the burdens and responsibilities of running a home, thousands of housewives in 1944 are war-workers too. They are doing a double job. They get no medals for it. But if ever women deserved especial honour, these do. So to all war-workers who also tackle shopping queues, cooking, cleaning, mending and the hundred and one other household jobs
Salute! FROM HOOVER
BY APPOINTMENT TO H.M. KING GEORGE VI AND H.M. QUEEN MARY
HOOVER LIMITED, PERIVALE, GREENFORD, MIDDLESEX

From Picture Post, *September 1944. What does this advertisement tell us about attitudes towards women's role in the home?*

SUFFERING, INCONVENIENCE AND LITTLE GLAMOUR

Mrs Briggs was an elderly woman whose house was bombed in an air-raid on a town in the south of England. Mrs Briggs could have been an elderly mother in Dresden or Dijon or Rome or Singapore or Tokyo or Rotterdam or Leningrad or just about anywhere that the bombers or the great artillery guns could reach:

Mrs Briggs is interviewed by a green-uniformed officer of the Assistance Board. Her hands are shaking. She doesn't know how to begin. He takes her name and address, particulars of the damage and her losses. Still Mrs Briggs doesn't quite know what to ask for. And then he says 'I suppose you'll be wanting some money to get started again?' She smiles and says 'Yes'. And then he says: 'What about clothes Mrs Briggs? Will you be wanting some coupons?' She leans forward confidentially and whispers that all her underclothes and nightclothes were buried in her bedroom. He understands and recommends a suitable number of coupons. . . . Mrs Briggs is moving off when a thought strikes her and she comes back embarrassed: 'My plate' she says to the Assistance Board Officer. He doesn't need any further explanation. He's heard it often before. Mrs Briggs didn't have time to put her dental plate in her mouth before the bomb fell. The officer makes arrangements for Mrs Briggs to have a new set made as quickly as possible. . . . Mrs Briggs pauses at the sign 'Billeting'. A sympathetic girl arranges a billet for her. Would Mrs Briggs like to be evacuated? 'Oh, No, Miss,' she answers. 'I want to be here when my sons come on leave. And I don't want them to know anything about all this either.'

(*Source: Picture Post*, 16 September 1944)

THINGS TO DO AND THINK ABOUT:

Think about the images you have of the Second World War. Divide them into opinions, judgments and facts.

From where have you derived most of your information: films, memories, books, comics, documentaries, etc? Divide your sources of information into primary and secondary sources and make an assessment of the reliability of each source.

Filling in the Background: The Treaty of Versailles

THE TREATY AND GERMANY

The Treaty of Versailles, which ended the First World War between Germany and the Allies, is often said to have been a root cause of the Second World War that engulfed Europe only twenty years later. The terms of the treaty were dictated to the new German government formed *after* the signing of the Armistice. Many of the members of this government had had little to do with the prosecution of the war. The Germans were not allowed to negotiate or modify the terms of the treaty. It was presented to them by the victorious nations as a *fait accompli* on 7 May 1919.

42. Germany is forbidden to maintain or construct any fortifications either on the left bank of the Rhine or on the right bank to the west of a line drawn fifty kilometers to the east of the Rhine.
43. In the area defined above the maintenance and the assembly of armed forces and military manoeuvres of any kind . . . are in the same way forbidden. . .
45. As compensation for the destruction of the coal mines in the North of France and as part payment towards the total reparation due from Germany for the damage resulting from the war, Germany cedes to France . . . the coal mines situated in the Saar basin. . .
51. The High Contracting Parties, recognizing the moral obligation to redress the wrong done by Germany in 1871 both to the rights of France and to the wishes of the population of Alsace Lorraine, which were separated from their country. . . The territories that were ceded to Germany . . . are restored to French sovereignty. . .
80. Germany acknowledges and will respect strictly the independence of Austria. . .
87. Germany recognizes the complete independence of Poland, and renounces in her favour all rights and title over the territory. . .
119. Germany renounces in favour of the Principal Allied and Associated Powers all her rights and titles over her overseas possessions. . .
160. The German Army must not exceed one hundred thousand men, including officers and establishments of depots. The Army shall be devoted exclusively to the maintenance of order within the territory and to the control of frontiers. . .
231. The Allied and Associated Governments affirm and Germany accepts the responsibility of Germany and her Allies for causing all the loss and damage to which the Allied and Associated Governments and their nationals have been subjected as a consequence of the war imposed upon them by the aggression of Germany and her Allies. . . . Germany undertakes that she will make compensation for all damage done to the civilian population of the Allied and Associated Powers and to their property.

(*Source:* The Treaty of Versailles)

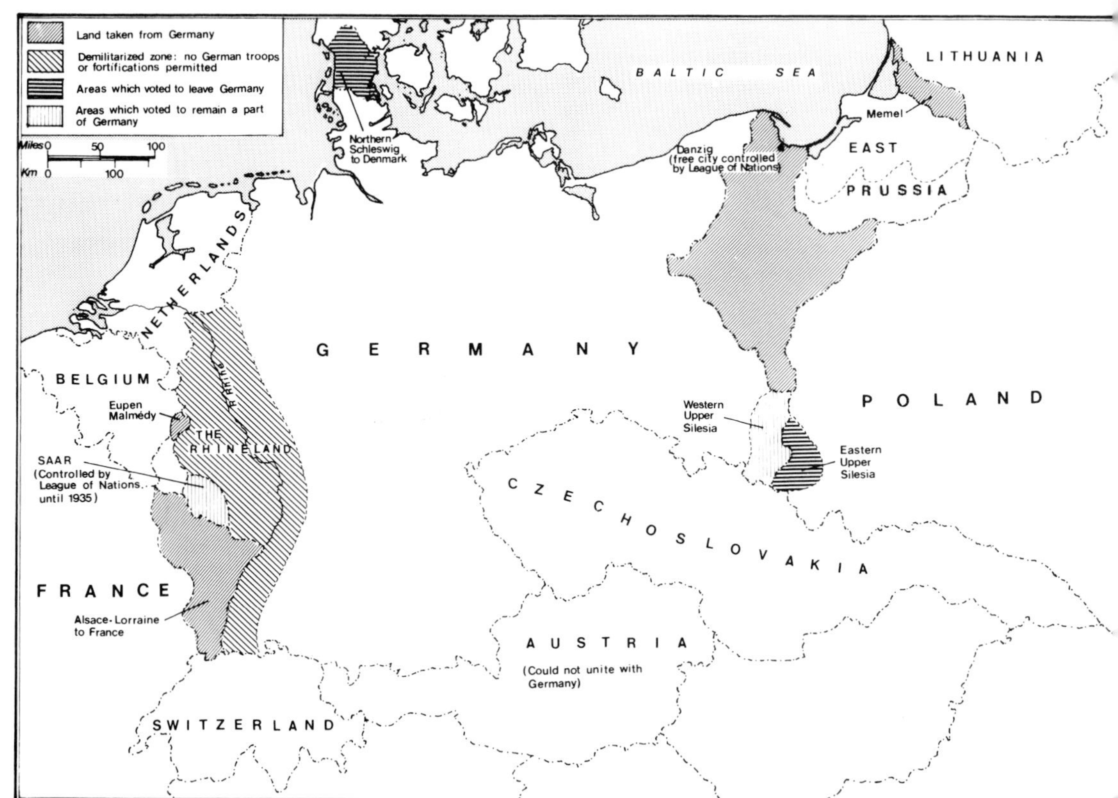

This map shows the effects of the Treaty of Versailles on German territory in Europe. Germany also lost all her colonies.

Which clauses of the treaty show the Allies' determination to limi Germany's territory?

Which clauses show the Allies' determination to limit Germany's armec forces?

Which clauses show the Allies' determination to make Germany pay for the war?

THE GERMAN VIEW OF VERSAILLES

German Cabinet Meeting, 21 March 1919:

Landsberg: The question of guilt and reparations cannot be separated. The march into Belgium resulted from an emergency but was not self-defence. Emergency conditions do not relieve us from the responsibility for damages so we should consent to make restitution. The payments should be small.
Ebert: What is the extreme limit of our capacity for reparations payments?
. . .
Erzberger: Let us maintain, according to the note of November 5 [1918 that reparations be limited to damage in occupied areas. No other demands should be recognized. . .
Count Rantzau: I agree. The Reich reparation commission has estimated that on that basis we would have to pay 20 to 25 billions. This takes into account deliveries since armistice and perhaps colonies given up. This

sum is within reason. Payments should be in kind.

(*Source:* Extracts from meeting of Reich Ministry, 21 March 1919, quoted in Hiden, *The Weimar Republic*, Longman, 1974)

When the German Cabinet was holding this conversation they had no idea what terms the Versailles Treaty would contain. Nor did they know that they were not allowed to negotiate those terms at all.

The German Delegation, Paris, 7 May 1919:

Gentlemen I am drunk. This shameful treaty has broken me. . . . Right now if I had those fellows here, who this afternoon were sitting opposite me – Wilson, Lloyd George, and Clemenceau – they would hit the ceiling so hard that they'd stick to it. But I am telling you this, gentlemen . . . if those fellows think that the German labourers are going to work hard for that capitalist gang, they're wrong, and when they march into the mining district, the few hand grenades that'll be needed to flood every mine will be on hand.

(*Source:* Luckau, The German Delegation to the Paris Peace Conference, Colombia University Press, 1941)

Can you account for the difference in view expressed in the last two extracts? Can both of them be regarded as reliable?

THE BRITISH VIEW OF THE PEACE

One man attending the Paris Peace Conference was a clever young economist, John Maynard Keynes. Convinced that the idea of funding all war damage out of reparations from the already ruined German economy would lead to economic disaster throughout Europe, he resigned his post as a civil servant and wrote a book called *The Economic Consequences of the Peace*. His ideas fell on fertile ground. Although the book attacked only

"PERHAPS IT WOULD GEE-UP BETTER IF WE LET IT TOUCH EARTH"

A British comment on reparations, from 1921. Do you think David Low had read or heard of Keynes's book on the peace treaties?

the reparation clauses, British public opinion extended Keyne's criticism to apply to the whole of the Treaty of Versailles.

Why do you think that was?

JAPAN: ONE OF THE VICTORS

Unlike other countries in the Far East, Japan had just been able to sustain independence from Western control. From the middle of the nineteenth century, the Japanese embarked on a policy of constructing an industrialized state that would continue to provide sufficient economic power to preserve that independence. In 1904 the success of this policy was marked by Japan's triumph over Russia in war.

The assumptions of the West are questioned:

It is sometimes said that Japan's victory [over Russia] spells the immediate rise of the yellow peril. She will reorganize China's military power; and raising her to the standard of her own efficient financial, educational and governmental attainments, will make those four hundred million people invincible . . . if might makes right for the white man why not for the yellow man? If Japan and China have the might, why should they not swagger and burn and kill and rule? We who are white have had the 'big head' badly for several centuries. Surely turn about would be but fair play.

(*Source:* L. Gullick, *The White Peril in the Far East*, New York, 1905)

In 1914, Japan entered the war on the side of the Allies and occupied German territory in China. At the Versailles Treaty negotiations, the Japanese delegation was treated with great courtesy and, as a reward for having participated in the struggle on the winning side, Japan received the League of Nations' mandate to administer the ex-German colonies of the Marianas, the Carolines and the Marshall Islands. Japanese holdings on the Chinese mainland, in the peninsula of Shantung, were bitterly contested by the Chinese, who had American support. The subsequent Treaty of Washington in 1922 returned the peninsula to China and Eastern Siberia to the Soviet Union.

THE LEAGUE OF NATIONS

The first clause of the Treaty of Versailles established the League of Nations, an organization of all the countries, which would help prevent another war happening. The League had a Covenant, that is, a list of rules and orders about its organization to which all members had to agree.

The Covenant:

Article 10. The members of the League undertake to respect and preserve as against external aggression the territorial integrity and existing political independence of all members of the League. In case of

THIS
LEAGUE OF NATIONS
BRIDGE
WAS DESIGNED BY
THE PRESIDENT OF THE
U·S·A·
BELGIUM
FRANCE
ENGLAND
ITALY
KEYSTONE
USA

THE GAP IN THE BRIDGE.

There was much dismay at the failure of the United States to ratify the treaty and join the League of Nations. This is a cartoon from Punch.

any such aggression or in case of any threat of danger of such aggression the council shall advise upon the means by which this obligation shall be fulfilled.

How did the supporters of the League of Nations hope that this clause would prevent war?

From the very beginning, the League of Nations was beset with problems. One of the most serious was that the United States would not ratify (or confirm) the Treaty of Versailles and thus the League.

America rejects the treaty:

. . . Upon agreeing to the resolution of ratification the yeas are 49 and the nays are 35. Not having received the affirmative votes of two thirds of the Senators present and voting, the resolution is not agreed to, and the senate does not advise and consent to the ratification of the treaty of peace with Germany. . .

Resolution of ratification

That the senate advise and consent to the ratification of the treaty . . . subject to the following [15] reservations. . .

2. The United States assumes no obligation to preserve the territorial integrity or political independence of any other country by the employment of its military or naval forces, its resources or any form of

economic discrimination, or to interfere in any way in controversies relating to territorial integrity or political independence, whether members of the League or not, under the provisions of Article 10 [of the Covenant], or to employ the military or naval forces of the United States, under any article of the Treaty for any purposes unless in a particular case the Congress, which, under the Constitution, has the sole power to declare war or authorize the employment of the military or naval forces of the United States, shall, in the exercise of full liberty of action, by Act or joint resolution so provide. . .

(*Source:* Resolution of Ratification of Treaty of Peace with Germany and the League of Nations, 19 March 1920)

THINGS TO DO AND THINK ABOUT:

What objections is the Senate expressing to Article 10?

Why does the British cartoonist see the US as the "Keystone to the Arch"?

PEACE AND FUTURE CANNON FODDER
1940 CLASS
PEACE TREATY
The Tiger: "Curious! I seem to hear a child weeping!"

A cartoon from the Daily Herald, *June 1919. This cartoon appears in many books about the causes of the Second World War. Why do you think it is chosen by historians? Is this cartoon really prophetic?*

Filling in the Background: Economic Relations

One consequence of the Versailles Treaty's declaration of Germany's war guilt was that Germany was required to pay reparations, or war damages, to the victorious countries. France, in particular, the country which had suffered the greatest losses, was determined that Germany should pay, and it was a popular theme at first, too, in British politics.

MAKE GERMANY PAY

The Reparations Commission set Germany's liability in 1920 at 132,000 million gold Marks, and laid down the rate at which she must repay this. At first, Germany managed to pay the debts as they became scheduled, but by early 1922 she could no longer pay. Britain was conscious that Germany's weak economic position was doing damage to her own economy, and therefore she wished to renegotiate the matter of reparations. However, France and Belgium declared Germany to be in breach of her obligations, and in January 1923 French troops occupied the Ruhr, Germany's industrial heartland. The consequences of this were not what the French had anticipated.

A German view of the French occupation of the Ruhr. Can you draw a cartoon which you think the French newspapers might have used?

PASSIVE RESISTANCE

For eight months the German people in the Ruhr kept up a passive resistance to those whom they saw as the invaders. They were supported and encouraged in this by the German government.

Proclamation calling off passive resistance:

On 11 January French troops occupied the German Ruhr territory. Since then the Ruhr territory and the Rhineland have had to suffer much oppression. Over 180,000 German men, women, old people and children have been driven from house and home. Millions of Germans no longer know what personal freedom is. Countless acts of violence have accompanied the occupation, more than one hundred fellow Germans have lost their lives, and hundreds are still languishing in prison. . .

The Reich government undertook to do what it could for the suffering compatriots. An ever-increasing amount of the means of the Reich has been claimed by this task. In the past week support for the Ruhr and the Rhineland amounted to 3500 billion marks. Economic life in Germany is disrupted. Perserverance on our present course threatens the terribly serious danger that it will be impossible to establish a stable currency, to maintain economic activity, and thus even to secure a bare existence for our people. . . . To save the life of the people and the state we face today the bitter necessity of breaking off the struggle.

(*Source:* German Government Proclamation, September 1923)

HYPER-INFLATION

The German economy was already in a state of collapse:

Number of Marks to buy 1 dollar's worth of goods:

Date	Marks per dollar
1914	4.2
1919	8.9
1921 (Nov)	70
1922 (Jan)	192
1922 (Aug)	1,000
1923 (Jan)	18,000
1923 (July)	160,000
1923 (August)	1,000,000
1923 (Nov)	4,200,000,000

Draw these figures in a line graph, which will give you a clearer idea of the extent of the problem.

Such inflation is called "hyper-inflation". The Mark note became completely worthless. Although the value of money was later re-established in Germany, the memories of these days in 1923 remained in people's consciousness for a very long time.

Making ends meet:

May I give you some recollections of my own situation at that time? As soon as I received my salary I rushed out to buy the daily necessities. My daily salary as editor of the periodical *Soziale Praxis*, was just enough to buy one loaf of bread and a small piece of cheese and some oatmeal. On one occasion I had to refuse to give a lecture at a Berlin city college because I could not be assured that my fee would cover the subway fare to the classroom and it was too far to walk. On another occasion, a private lesson I gave to the wife of a farmer was paid somewhat better – by one loaf of bread for the hour.

An acquaintance of mine, a clergyman, came to Berlin from a suburb with his monthly salary to buy a pair of shoes for his baby; he could buy only a cup of coffee. The Zeiss works in Jena, a non-profit enterprise, calculated the gold-mark equivalent of its average wage paid during a week in November 1923 and found weekly earnings to be worth four gold marks, less than a sixth of prewar levels.

(*Source:* Dr Frieda Wunderlich, quoted in Bry, *Wages in Germany 1871-1945*, Princeton, 1960

Starvation threatens:

It is understandable that . . . health levels are deteriorating ever more seriously. While the figures for the Reich as a whole are not yet available, we do have a preliminary mortality rate for towns with 100,000 or more inhabitants. After having fallen in 1920-21, it has climbed again for the year 1921-22, rising from 12.6 to 13.4 per thousand inhabitants. In 1922 those familiar diseases appeared again in increasing numbers which attack a people when it is suffering from insufficient nutrition, when it also can no longer obtain the other necessities of life. Thus edema is re-appearing, the so-called war-dropsy, which is a consequence of a bad and overly-watery diet. There are increases in stomach disorders and food poisoning, which are the result of eating spoiled foods. There are complaints of the appearance of scurvy, which is a consequence of an unbalanced and improper diet. From various parts of the Reich, reports are coming in about an increase in suicides. . . . More and more often one finds 'old age' and 'weakness' listed in these official records on the causes of death; these are equivalent to death through hunger.

(*Source:* speech to the Reichstag by President of the Department of Health, 20 February 1923, quoted in Ringer, *The German Inflation of 1923*, OUP, 1969)

In what ways might these sorts of experiences have affected the way people thought and felt?

AMERICA PAYS

International pressure was brought to bear on France to find some long-term solution to the reparations problem. A committee, under the chairmanship of an American banker, Charles Dawes, met in 1924 and drew up a plan by which Germany would be lent about 800 million gold Marks to help her make her repayments, and the schedule for repayments was altered. Most of the money needed was to be lent by the United States.

Economic order was re-established in Germany, accompanied by political stability, and Germany returned steadily to the centre of European affairs. In 1925 Germany signed the Treaty of Locarno as an equal with France, Britain, Belgium and Italy, and in 1926 she was admitted into the League of Nations. As this happened, Germany's high interest rates and low wage rates made her an attractive investment prospect, particularly for the surplus capital that was being produced by the booming American economy. America may have made a decision to withdraw from European politics, but her position as a major manufacturing and industrial nation with trading links throughout the world meant that her isolation was only skin-deep. Her economic involvement in Europe was enormous and in Germany the greatest of all.

THE WALL STREET CRASH

In the summer of 1929 ominous signs began to appear on the economic horizon. Unemployment began to creep up in Germany. In the United States the rate of new building began to slow down. Two years of wonderful harvests had lowered the price of grain to the point where the incomes of farmers were falling too low to allow them to buy as many manufactured goods as they had been doing. In October the price of shares began to fall and on 24 October they fell so far and so fast that there was a huge crisis of confidence in the American economy. Millions of ordinary people lost their savings when the price of shares fell.

Unemployed in the USA:

Then began the daily disheartening tramp for a job. Every morning at six and sometimes earlier he was out. His was always a very meagre breakfast, often only a piece of bread and later there was not enough even of that for him and the kids, so he went without. This was in winter. Once in a while he picked up a job shovelling snow or cleaning snow from the streets. This helped a little with food but not nearly enough. The children began to lose weight and soon looked pale. His wife was not well and became more and more nervous with the strain. The rent was past due two months and the landlady knocked each morning at the door demanding payments: the gas man knocked: the electric man came: the furniture collector followed. A knock became symbolical of their distress. Then everything fell at once. First came a five day notice to quit their house; then the gas was shut off; then the electricity; then came a telegram demanding payment on the furniture; then the insurance lapsed. The grocery man, when he found that Pavlowski had no work refused further credit.

(*Source:* Marion Elerton, *Case Studies of Unemployment*)

FROM AMERICA TO THE REST OF THE WORLD

In an attempt to meet the demands being made on them for funds, the American banks called in the loans which they had made throughout the world. The withdrawal of capital from Germany, Japan, Britain, France – everywhere – extended the effects of the collapse of the American economy to every country. Even the Soviet Union, normally insulated from the vagaries of capitalism, was affected by the very low prices available for corn in the international markets. World trade collapsed, German banks failed, unemployment rose.

SOME EFFECTS OF THE WORLDWIDE DEPRESSION

Unemployment in Germany, 1928-32:

Date	Number of unemployed
1928	1,862,000
1929	2,850,000
1930	3,217,000
1931	4,886,000
1932	6,042,000

Unemployment in Britain, 1928-32:

Date	% of workforce unemployed
1928	10.7
1929	10.3
1930	15.8
1931	21.1
1932	21.9

Price of Japanese raw silk thread (mostly exported to USA):

Date	Price per 60 kilos in Yen
Dec. 1929	Y1,174
June 1930	Y849
Dec. 1930	Y625
June 1931	Y527

The international economic system was badly shaken. Countries retreated behind closed doors. The international gold standard, which had controlled the exchange of currencies, was abandoned by many. Trade shrank and, as countries tried to defend their own industries from cheap imports, barriers of every description were raised against trade. The answer seemed to lie in economic self-sufficiency – controlling sufficient supplies of your own raw materials and food stuffs to provide for your own people's needs. Since dependence on other countries' economic health (particularly that of the United States) had brought about the disaster of 1929, only independence from such forces would ensure that such disaster could not strike again. This economic nationalism fitted well with the aggressive political nationalism that was also developing in the 1920s.

THINGS TO DO AND THINK ABOUT:

Transfer the statistical information on to a graph. Work out three judgments you can make about the possible effects of these changes.

Why would the experience of 1923 have created particular problems for Germany when the Depression came?

Filling in the Background: Ideas in Action

NEW IDEAS IN GERMANY

On 30 January 1933 a new Chancellor took office in Germany. His name was Adolf Hitler and he was the leader of the National Socialist Party of Germany, commonly known as the Nazi Party.

The Nazi Party is often referred to as a fascist party – fascism being a set of political ideas that had developed in the early years of the twentieth century. In some ways Naziism *was* a fascist ideology, in the emphasis it put on action and state power, but it was also more than that, particularly in its analysis of race. In fact, National Socialism was primarily the ideology of one man, and his writings can give us the clearest picture of it.

Living space:

. . . We national socialists must hold unflinchingly to our aim in foreign policy, namely to secure for the German people the land and soil to which they are entitled on this earth. And this action is the only one which, before God and our German posterity, would make any sacrifice of blood seem justified: before God, since we have been put on this earth with the mission of eternal struggle for our daily bread, beings who receive nothing as a gift, and who owe their position as lords of the earth only to the genius and the courage with which they can conquer and defend it. . . . The soil on which some day German generations of peasants can beget powerful sons will sanction the investment of the sons of today, and will some day acquit the responsible statesmen of blood-guilt. . .

(*Source:* Adolf Hitler, *Mein Kampf*, 1924)

A programme for power:

. . . 2. Foreign Policy: Battle against Versailles. Equality of right in Geneva; but useless if people do not have the will to fight. . .
3. Economics: The farmer must be saved! Settlement Policy! Further increase of exports useless. . . . The only possibility of re-employing part of the army of unemployed lies in settlement . . . living space too small for German people.
4. Building up the armed forces: Most important pre-requisite for achieving the goal of regaining political power. . .
How should political power be used when it has been gained? . . . Perhaps fighting for new export possibilities, perhaps – and probably better – the conquest of new living space in the east and its ruthless Germanization. . .

(*Source:* Notes of Hitler's first speech to generals of the German Army, 3 February 1933)

Given what you know about German history since 1919, why might some of these ideas have appealed to German people?

THE BATTLE AGAINST VERSAILLES

One of the central aims of the Nazi Party's policy was to reverse the terms of the Treaty of Versailles. Hitler and his party had come to national prominence in a vigorous campaign against the terms of the Young Plan, a "new deal" on reparations negotiated with the Allies in 1929. The Depression followed close on the heels of this campaign and the Nazi Party grew from strength to strength. Hitler's simple argument – that the humiliation of Versailles was the reason for Germany's present troubles and that the only way for the country to return to greatness was to overthrow the treaty – produced a popular response in the German people.

GERMANY RE-ARMS

In 1933 Germany withdrew from the League of Nations and began a programme of re-armament. This was openly declared in 1935, when conscription was introduced. The ideas at work were those which Hitler had outlined in *Mein Kampf* and in his speech to the generals. To be great, Germany must be strong; to be strong meant a large army; to be strong meant asserting one's rights and rejecting the Treaty of Versailles.

WHAT SHOULD BRITAIN DO?

Foreign Office, 29 November 1934:

a) Are we prepared to contemplate the legalization of German armaments?
b). . .What is our line going to be when Germany either demands their legalization or announces that she has armed in violation of the Treaty of Versailles, and intends to continue to disregard the treaty?
. . .the best course would be to recognize that Germany's re-armament in breach of the Treaty is a fact which cannot be altered and to reach the conclusion that this had better be recognized without delay in the hope that we can still get, in return for legalization, some valuable terms from Germany.

A view of the crowd at a Nazi meeting in the Lustgarten, Berlin, during Hitler's May Day speech, 2 May 1939. What sort of atmosphere do you think might have prevailed at a meeting like this?

. . .I cannot think that British public opinion will remain satisfied with the futility of ignoring the facts that German armaments are in breach of the Treaty. Once it is avowed that they are and admitted on all hands this cannot be prevented, there will be an increasing demand to get rid of the lumber while it may still fetch a price. . .
J.S.

(*Source:* Memo from Sir John Simon, British Foreign Secretary)

This was a private memo. Do you think that it is more reliable as a source of information than a public statement? Why or why not?

PAX GERMANICA
LOCARNO
Ernest H. Shepard
THE GOOSE-STEP.
"GOOSEY GOOSEY GANDER,
WHITHER DOST THOU WANDER?"
"ONLY THROUGH THE RHINELAND—
PRAY EXCUSE MY BLUNDER!"

A cartoon from Punch, *March 1936. Why has the cartoonist portrayed Germany as a goose?*

GERMANY RECLAIMS THE RHINELAND

In March 1936 the German army re-occupied the Rhineland, which the Treaty of Versailles had designated a de-militarized zone.

THINGS TO DO AND THINK ABOUT:

What image is the cartoonist trying to convey of Germany in 1936? Do you think this image is supported by the writings of Hitler?

What policy is Sir John Simon advocating as a reaction to Germany's planned re-armament?

NEW IDEAS IN JAPAN

In the second half of the nineteenth century Japanese leaders adopted a policy of modernization for their country. In this way they hoped to resist the pressures that the powerful Western nations were putting on Japan to submit to their economic (if not political) control. In order to create a new kind of society which would encourage industrialization and increase Japanese wealth, the Japanese leaders made new laws. However, these new laws were couched in the traditions, language and ideas of the past.

Meiji statement on education:

Know Ye, Our Subjects:
Our Imperial Ancestors have founded Our Empire on a basis broad and everlasting and have deeply and firmly implanted virtue; Our subjects ever united in filial piety have from generation to generation illustrated the beauty thereof. This is the glory of the fundamental character of Our Empire and herein also lies the source of our education. Ye, Our subjects, be filial to your parents, affectionate to your brothers and sisters; as husbands and wives be harmonious; as friends be true; bear yourselves in modesty and moderation; extend your benevolence to all; pursue learning and cultivate arts, and thereby develop intellectual faculties and perfect moral powers; furthermore, advance public good and promote common interests; always respect the Constitution and observe the laws; should emergency arise, offer yourselves courageously to the State; and thus guard and maintain the prosperity of Our Imperial Throne coevel [i.e. equal] with heaven and earth. So shall ye not only be Our good and faithful subjects, but render illustrious the best traditions of your fore-fathers.

The Way here set forth is indeed the teaching bequeathed by Our Imperial Ancestors to be observed alike by their Descendants and their subjects, infallible for all ages and true in all places. It is Our wish to lay it to heart in all reverence in common with you, Our subjects, that we may attain the same virtue.

(*Source:* Meiji statement of education, 1890 – an Imperial Rescript read regularly thereafter to school children all over the country)

This is an example of *Kokutai*: the word used to describe the thinking and ideology behind the distinctive character of Japan's institutions and processes of government. *Kokutai* meant wedding together the past and the innovation the country needed.

As the pace of industrialization quickened, the institutions constructed to manage the change came increasingly under strain. The 1920s were a particularly difficult time. In 1922 the Treaty of Washington limited Japan's territorial gains from the First World War and put a curb on her attempts to take the lead in the international competition for the control of China. The size of her navy was limited compared with those of Britain and the USA. A devastating earthquake in 1923 killed over 100,000 people.

As the industrialization of Japan developed, so did her working class, who began to explore the challenging ideas of Marxism. These ideas were a threat to the traditional thinking of Japan's ruling class. China was struggling towards unification under a nationalist government, and Japan felt that her domination in the Far East might be affected. Finally, the effects of the Wall Street crash devastated Japan's economy.

All this fed an aggressive right-wing nationalist movement which had, at its centre, the younger members of the officer corps in the army. After 1930 *Kokutai*, which had served so successfully in adapting Japan's economy and social organization to the twentieth century, became the dogma of extreme nationalism and totalitarianism. It was easy to disguise what were, in fact, new ideas in the powerful language of the past. The Ancestor worship of Shinto, the ancient Japanese religion, became elevated into a cult, and the reverence for the Imperial family and the person of the Emperor, which had been the cornerstone on which the modernization programmes had been built, now became the wall behind which aggressive nationalist policies could be pursued with vigour.

THINGS TO DO AND THINK ABOUT:

Read the Imperial Rescript on Education and identify which aspects were designed to appeal to traditional ideas and which aspects were intended to encourage new ones.

The Rescript was read daily to children in Japanese schools. How might this have helped those who wanted to have the unquestioning support of the people for aggressive foreign adventures?

MANCHURIA INVADED

For some time Japan had held control over the railway system of Manchuria, one of the provinces of China. For some young officers, extending Japan's control over this province could only strengthen her position in the Far East.

SHELLING OF MUKDEN
REPORTED ATTACK BY JAPANESE
MANY CASUALTIES
From our correspondent

Peking September 18

A squad of Japanese soldiers approached the north camp at Mukden about 10 o'clock last night and opened fire on the camp. This was followed by shell-fire on the camp, the arsenal and the city from the Japanese concession. A message received here by Chang Hsueh-liang, the Governor of Manchuria, stated that at one o'clock the firing was still going on, one shell every 10 minutes. The Japanese Consular authorities were reported to be unable to induce the military to cease firing. The Chinese did not retaliate. . .

(*Source: The Times*, 19 September 1931)

MANCHURIAN FIGHTING
CAUSE OF THE OUTBREAK
JAPANESE ACCOUNT
From our own correspondent

Tokyo September 20

Within eighteen hours after Chinese soldiers had damaged the railway line, Japanese troops had not only occupied Mukden, but secured both ends of the South Manchuria Line by disarming the Chinese troops stationed at the Changchin and Newchwang terminals. . .

It is scarcely an exaggeration to say that Japanese Foreign Office Officials were stunned by the news. . .

Diplomatic officials stated that it was not intended to hold Mukden as a pawn in the settlement of the Manchurian problem, but that it would be evacuated as soon as conditions permitted. A high military official today informed me that the Army concurred in that view. . . . It must be added that many well-informed Japanese believe that Mukden should be held till Japan's grievances have been redressed. Several newspapers today declare that the Army correctly interpreted the sentiment of the nation. . .

(*Source: The Times*, 21 September 1931)

In March 1932 Manchuria was established as a new state called Manchukuo, a client state of Japan.

THINGS TO DO AND THINK ABOUT:

"The Manchurian crisis demonstrated the strength of the military in both military and political affairs": Can you find any evidence that supports this from the newspaper reports?

How do you account for the difference between the newspaper reports?

Filling in the Background: The End of the League of Nations

In 1929 work began on the building of the magnificent Palace of Nations, the headquarters of the League of Nations in Geneva.

When the Japanese army invaded Manchuria in 1931, the Chinese government reported the Japanese to the League of Nations. Events like those in Manchuria – where two member nations engaged in an act of war or aggression – were apparently exactly one kind of circumstances in which the League had been designed to act. The League dispatched a Commission of Enquiry, under Lord Lytton, to Manchuria to establish the facts.

Report of the Commission of Enquiry, February 1933:

. . .An explosion undoubtedly occurred on or near the railroad between 10 and 10.30 p.m. on September 18th, but the damage, if any, to the railroad did not, in fact prevent the punctual arrival of the southbound train from Changchun, and was not in itself sufficient to justify military action. The military operations of the Japanese troops during the night . . . cannot be regarded as measures of legitimate self-defence. . .

(*Source:* quoted in Maki, *Conflict and Tension in the Far East – Key Documents 1894-1960*, University of Washington Press, 1961)

The Japanese government's response to the Enquiry:

. . .the report adopted by the assembly at the special session of February 24th last, entirely misapprehending the spirit of Japan, pervaded as it is by no other desire than the maintenance of peace in the Orient, contains gross errors both in the ascertainment of facts and in the conclusions deduced.

(*Source:* Tokyo, 27 March 1933)

The League endorsed the Lytton report, and, as a result, Japan simply left the League. Weakened by this, the League was then effectively killed off by the next major problem it faced.

ITALY AND ABYSSINIA

In 1922 the Italian government had been taken over by the leader of the Italian Fascist Party, Benito Mussolini. He had followed a vigorous policy integrating the organizations of society (for instance, trade unions) into those of the state, as fascist theory dictated. By the mid-1930s he had become accepted by the Vatican and the landed families of Italy, and was looking to recreate the days of Rome's greatness by building an empire abroad. One of the few places left that had not been annexed by one or other of the European powers was Abyssinia, an independent African state of ancient foundation.

From late 1934, Mussolini began making such extreme demands on

Abyssinia that no-one was in any doubt that Italy was going to annex the state. The British government was certainly aware of what was now intended, and of what the consequences would be.

RITAIN AND THE ABYSSINIA QUESTION

. . .The position is as plain as a pikestaff. Italy will have to be bought off – let us use and face ugly words – in some form or other, or Abyssinia will eventually perish. That might in itself matter less, if it did not mean that the League would also perish (and that Italy would simultaneously perform ANOTHER volte-face into the arms of Germany. . .)

I agree that we cannot trade Abyssinia. . .

If we are all clear and in unison about that, it follows clearly that either there has got to be a disastrous explosion – that will wreck the League and very possibly His Majesty's Government too, if the League is destroyed on the eve of an election – or else that we have got to pay the price.
Foreign Office, 8 June 1935

(*Source:* Sir Robert Vansittart, Permanent Under Secretary at the Foreign Office, to the Foreign Secretary and Minister for League Affairs)

THE BRITISH EOPLE AND THE LEAGUE

A Peace Ballot was organized by the League of Nations Union, in an effort to publicize the amount of support that existed for the League. Eleven and a half million people in Britain were balloted.

The Peace Ballot, 1935:

Question 1: Should Great Britain remain a member of the League of Nations?

Total YES answers	10,642,560
Total NO answers	337,964
Percentage of YES answers in relation to total YES and NO answers	97.0
Percentage of YES answers in relation to total YES, NO and DOUBTFUL answers and abstentions	96.0

Question 5a: Do you consider that, if a nation insists on attacking another, the other nations should combine to compel it to stop by economic and non-military measures?

Total YES answers	9,627,606
Total NO answers	607,165
Percentage of YES answers in relation to total YES and NO answers	94.1
Percentage of YES answers in relation to total YES, NO, DOUBTFUL and CHRISTIAN PACIFIST answers and ABSTENTIONS	86.8

Question 5b: Do you consider that, if a nation insists on attacking another, the other nations should combine to compel it to stop by, if necessary, military measures?

Total YES answers	6,506,777
Total NO answers	2,262,261

Percentage of YES answers in relation to total YES and NO answers	74
Percentage of YES answers in relation to total YES, NO, DOUBTFUL and CHRISTIAN PACIFIST answers and ABSTENTIONS	58.

(*Source:* quoted in Livingstone, *The Peace Ballot*, Gollancz, 1935)

Had Vansittart read public opinion correctly?

BRITISH POLICY, AUGUST 1935

. . .Most people are still convinced that if we stick to the covenant and apply collective sanctions, Italy must give in and there will be no war. You and I know that the position is not as simple as this and that the presumption that firstly, there will be collective action . . . and secondly

THE AWFUL WARNING.

FRANCE AND ENGLAND (*together?*). "WE DON'T WANT YOU TO FIGHT, BUT, BY JINGO, IF YOU DO, WE SHALL PROBABLY ISSUE A JOINT MEMORANDUM SUGGESTING A MILD DISAPPROVAL OF YOU."

A cartoon from Punch, *1935. How does the cartoonist suggest that Britain and France are not particularly threatening?*

that economic sanctions will be effective are, to say the least, very bold and sanguine. None the less, whatever may develop it is essential that we should play out the League hand in September. . . . It must be the League and not the British Government that declares that sanctions are impracticable and the British Government must on no account lay itself open to the charge that we have not done our utmost to make them practicable. . .

(*Source:* Sir Samuel Hoare, Foreign Secretary, to British Ambassador in Paris, 24 August 1935)

At the League of Nations it had been agreed for some time that the most effective way to ensure collective security, as agreed in Article 10 of the Convention (see page 14), was to place a ban on trade and contact with any member state contravening the Article. These embargoes or trade bans are called sanctions. On 3 October 1935 Italian troops invaded Abyssinia. The League of Nations imposed limited sanctions; there was no ban on the sale to Italy of oil, coal, iron or steel.

In May 1936 the Italian army entered Addis Ababa and Mussolini announced the creation of the new Italian Empire.

In 1936, too, the new building – the Palace of Nations – was complete, but by then the League was discredited, Britain and France were following policies based on the pre-war principles of great power politics, and the collective security which the League had envisaged was a dead letter.

THINGS TO DO AND THINK ABOUT:

Does the Peace Ballot confirm Hoare's view that British policy must be seen to support the League?

What do you think might have been the significance of the answer to question 5b in the Peace Ballot?

Why was the League of Nations such a failure in the Manchurian and Abyssinian crises?

Into War: Europe, 1937-39

By the summer of 1937 the collective security system which the League of Nations had been designed to implement was dead. All over the world, in the aftermath of the First World War and the Wall Street Crash, people had turned to aggressive nationalist parties to lead them out of their difficulties. The Versailles Treaty was recognized as a dead letter by all the powers who carried any weight in the councils of the world. Hitler's re-armament programme and the re-occupation of the Rhineland confirmed this. Britain and France now pursued a foreign policy that openly reverted to the nineteenth-century idea of maintaining a balance of power between the nations of Europe and European control overseas. The League entered no one's calculations any more.

All these things formed the framework within which the events of the next four years took place. However, they do not in themselves constitute sufficient causes for the war. It was not inevitable, or even very likely, in the first half of 1937, that there would be a major war within two years. There is, though, a growing agreement among historians that, by the close of 1937, war had become much more likely – a real possibility. 1937 was a turning point; from then on, the immediate origins of the war can be discerned.

ENGLAND AND FRANCE IN 1937

France, who had been the most determined advocate of the harsh terms of the Treaty of Versailles and since then the most suspicious and sceptical observer of German policy, was severely weakened by her failure to act when Hitler re-militarized the Rhineland. Publicly, her politicians had been asserting that France would not stand idly by and watch the Treaty's protection of the Rhineland tossed aside – it was essential for French security. In the event, France did nothing – was unable and unwilling to do anything. It was now clear that Britain would have to take the lead in any stand against Hitler.

CHAMBERLAIN IN OFFICE

In May 1937 a new British Prime Minister took office. His name was Neville Chamberlain. It is he who is most closely associated with the policy of appeasement. It used to be believed that this was *his* policy, first enacted in 1937, but in fact, the ideas behind policy dated back to 1919. It aimed to reconcile the four leading European powers of France, Britain, Germany and Italy, with a view to securing general disarmament and a balance of interests within Europe. The new Prime Minister of Britain *did* pursue the policy with extra vigour and personal commitment, and this led to a new policy of British involvement in Eastern Europe – an involvement which was to lead to war.

Neville Chamberlain's view of Germany and Hitler:

26 November 1937
. . .the German visit [of Lord Halifax; a cabinet colleague] was from my

point of view a great success, because it achieved its object, that of creating an atmosphere in which it is possible to discuss with Germany the practical questions involved in a European settlement. . . . Both Hitler and Goering said separately and emphatically, that they had no desire or intention of making war, and I think we may take this as correct at least for the present. Of course they want to dominate Eastern Europe; they want as close a union with Austria as they can get without incorporating her into the Reich, and they want much the same thing for the Sudetendeutsche as we did for the Uitlanders in the Transvaal.

. . .Hitler was rather non-committal about disarmament, he did declare himself in favour of the abolition of bombing aeroplanes.

Now here, it seems to me, is a fair basis of discussion, though no doubt all these points bristle with difficulties. But I don't see why we shouldn't say to Germany, 'give us satisfactory assurances that you won't use force to deal with the Austrians and Czechoslovakians and we will give you similar assurances that we won't use force to prevent the changes you want if you can get them by peaceful means.'

(*Source:* Private diaries, quoted in Keith Feiling, *The Life of Neville Chamberlain*, London, 1946)

ERMANY IN 1937

In November 1937 Hitler held a meeting with the chief officers of the German armed forces to discuss the direction of German foreign affairs and re-armament over the following years. The following extract is from the notes made of the meeting by one of those present, Colonel Hossbach.

THE HOSSBACH MEMORANDUM

Planning the future:

Minutes of the Conference in the Reich Chancellery, Berlin, November 5 1937 from 4:15 to 8:30 p.m.

Present: The Führer and Chancellor
Field Marshall von Blomberg, War Minister,
Colonel General Baron von Fritsch, Commander in Chief, Army
Admiral Dr H.C. Raeder, Commander in Chief, Navy
Colonel General Göring, Commander in Chief, Luftwaffe
Baron von Neurath, Foreign Minister
Colonel Hossbach

The Führer began by stating that the subject of the present conference was of such importance that its discussion would, in other countries certainly be a matter for a full cabinet meeting, but he, the Führer, had rejected the idea of making it a subject of discussion before the wider circle of the Reich's cabinet just because of the importance of the matter. . .

The aim of German policy was to make secure and to preserve the racial community and to enlarge it. It was therefore a question of space. . . . German policy had to reckon with two hate-inspired antagonists, Britain and France, to whom a German colossus in the centre of Europe was a thorn in the flesh. . .

Germany's problem could only be solved by means of force and this was never without attendant risk. . . . If one accepts as the basis of the following exposition the resort to force with its attendant risks, then there remain still to be answered the questions 'when' and 'how'. . .

. . .1943-1945
After this date only a change for the worse, from our point of view, could be expected.
. . .Our relative strength would decrease in relation to the rearmament which would, by then, have been carried out by the rest of the world. . .

If the Führer was still living it was his unalterable resolve to solve Germany's problem of space at the latest by 1943-45. . .

For the improvement of our political-military position our first objective, in the event of being embroiled in war, must be to overthrow Czechoslovakia and Austria simultaneously. . .
The Führer believed that almost certainly Britain and probably France as well, had tacitly written off the Czechs and were reconciled to the fact tha this question would be cleared up in due course by Germany. . .
The incorporation of these two states with Germany meant a substantia advantage because it would mean shorter and better frontiers, the freeing of forces for other purposes and the possibility of creating new units up to a level of about 12 divisions. . .

(*Source:* quoted in *Documents on German Foreign Policy 1919-1945*)

THINGS TO DO AND THINK ABOUT:

Compare the documents of Chamberlain's and Hitler's views. Do the agree with each other? In what ways?

Chamberlain's ideas were written later than the memorandum. Does th mean that he should have known what was in Hitler's address to th group?

Early in 1938 Hitler dismissed Blomberg and Fritsch and replaced ther with himself and leading members of the Nazi Party. Both of them ha urged caution at the Hossbach meeting. What conclusions could you dra from the dismissals?

GERMAN EXPANSION

During the First World War, Austria-Hungary, then one of the great power of Europe, had fought with Germany against the Allies. Following he defeat, at the treaty negotiations in Paris Austria's empire was taken fror her. She asked to be united with Germany, arguing that the people had th right to decide for themselves which country they wished to belong to. Thi idea of self-determination, expounded by President Wilson, was bein used to justify the creation of new European states. However, Austria'

INCREASING PRESSURE

What message is this cartoon by David Low trying to convey? How reliable are cartoons as vidence of (a) what people nderstood was happening, and (b) what was really happening? From right to left, the rushed figures are labelled: Austria, Czech, Balkans, Near East, N.W. Europe, France, Britain. Britain's basket is labelled The British Empire.

request was denied by the Allies, who were anxious to prevent Germany emerging again as the dominant European power.

Unification, or *Anschluss*, with Germany remained a goal of Austrian political organizations until 1933, when the Nazi Party came to power. By then, many Europeans and leading politicians in the Allied countries, in their general questioning of the Treaty of Versailles, had come to accept the legitimacy of Austrian wishes and regretted the decision of 1919 to prevent unification. In his comments on Lord Halifax's visit to Germany in November 1937 Chamberlain noted that Germany wanted as close a union as possible with Austria, without actually annexing her.

As the nature of the Nazi government had become clear, both leading Austrian political parties had removed *Anschluss* from their manifestos, but Hitler, himself an Austrian, was determined to bring the two countries closer together. The Austrian Nazi Party, funded and directed from Berlin, became more and more powerful. In a desperate attempt to preserve Austrian independence, the Chancellor, Schuschnigg, decided to ask the Austrian people, in a plebiscite, to pass judgment on the question of *Anschluss*. If the people rejected *Anschluss*, Hitler's claims for Austria could no longer be seen as legitimate. In panic, Hitler invaded on 12 March 1938 and the next day declared the incorporation of Austria into the *Reich*. Not a shot was fired, and although Britain and France delivered protests to the German government, they had long expected the *Anschluss* and suspected that, in principle, it was right.

GERMAN EXPANSION: CZECHOSLOVAKIA

Czechoslovakia was a country that had been created by the Treaty of Versailles, mostly out of the former Austria-Hungarian Empire. Its population consisted of a number of different nationalities, illustrated by these census figures from 1930:

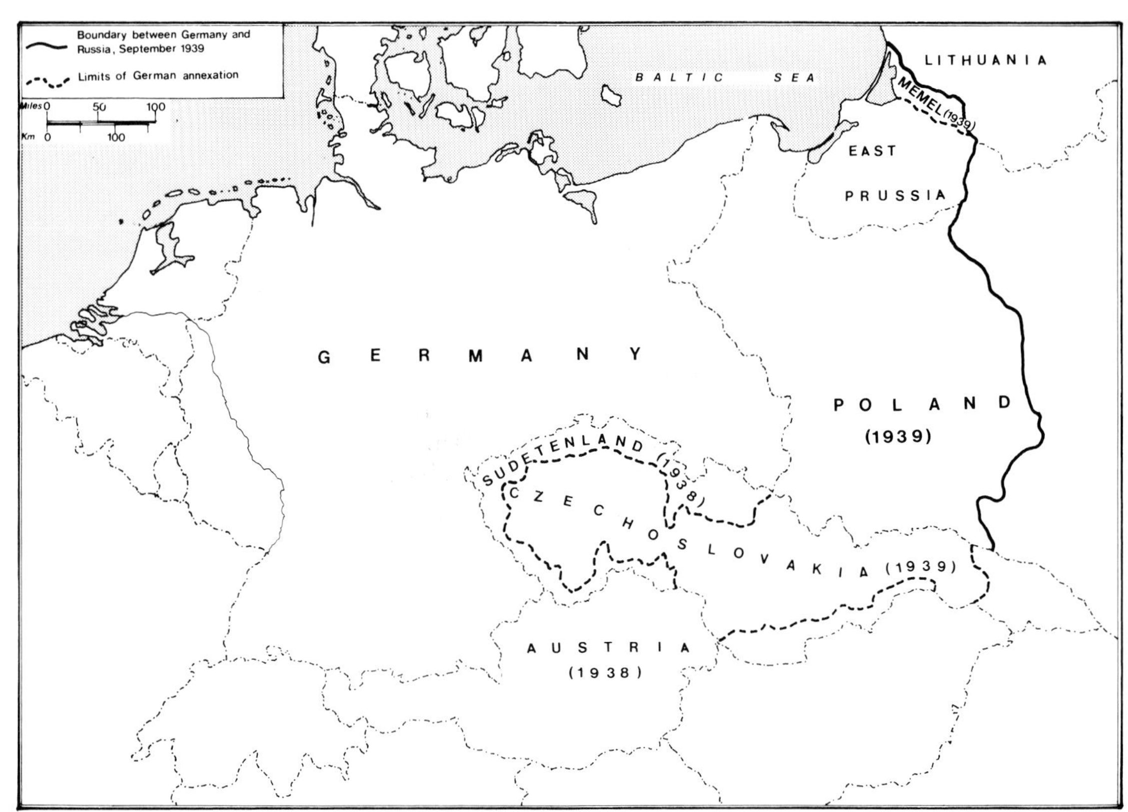

This map shows the expansion of German territory between 1938 and 1939. Compare it to the map of the Versailles Settlement on page 12.

Czechs	7,447,000
Germans	3,218,000
Slovaks	2,309,000
Magyars	720,000
Ruthenes	569,000
Poles	100,000
Others	266,000

Most of the Germans in Czechoslovakia lived in a horseshoe-shaped area along the frontier with Germany and Austria, called the Sudetenland (see the map above). Before the first World War these Germans had been the most powerful in Bohemia. In the 1920s, they found themselves instead having to take second place to the Czechs in the new state. Despite this, it looked as though the majority of German citizens were adapting successfully and participating fully in the life of Czechoslovakia. Then, in 1930, the process of assimilating them into the country was checked, with the onset of the great Depression. The Depression hit Czechoslovakia hard and the rural population of Sudetenland even harder. The government in Prague was blamed for the difficulties and, seeing an apparent economic miracle going on just over the border in Germany, many Sudeten Germans began to support the Nazi Party. They began to demand unification with Germany, with Hitler's full support. The *Anschluss* provided an enormous boost to the Sudeten Nazi Party, whose membership increased to 1.3 million in the months around March 1938. Everyone recognized that Hitler's next territorial demands would centre around the issue of Sudetenland.

Britain and Czechoslovakia:

20 March
. . .You have only to look at the map to see that nothing that France or we could do could possibly save Czechoslovakia from being overrun by the Germans if they wanted to do it. The Austrian frontier is practically open; the great Skoda munitions works are within easy bombing distance of the German aerodromes, the railways all pass through German territory, Russia is 100 miles away. Therefore we could not help Czechoslovakia – she would simply be a pretext for going to war with Germany. That we could not think of unless we had a reasonable prospect of being able to beat her to her knees in a reasonable time, and of that I see no sign. I have therefore abandoned any idea of giving guarantees to Czechoslovakia, or the French in connection with her obligations to that country.

(*Source:* Private diaries, quoted in Keith Feiling, *The Life of Neville Chamberlain*, London, 1946)

Hitler and Czechoslovakia:

TOP SECRET MILITARY BERLIN, MAY 30, 1938
. . .By order of the Supreme Commander of the Wehrmacht . . . part . . . of the directive on the combined preparations for war . . . is to be replaced by the attached version. Its execution must be assured by October 1, 1938, at the latest. . .
WAR ON TWO FRONTS WITH MAIN EFFORT IN SOUTHEAST (STRATEGIC CONCENTRATION GREEN)

1 Political Assumptions
It is my unalterable decision to smash Czechoslovakia by military action in the near future. . .

An unavoidable development of events within Czechoslovakia, or other political events in Europe providing a suddenly favourable opportunity which may never recur, may cause me to take early action. . .

(*Source:* Orders from Hitler to the Wehrmacht, quoted in *Documents on German Foreign Policy, 1919-1945*)

France and Czechoslovakia:

France had a treaty with Czechoslovakia guaranteeing to go to her aid if she were attacked by another country. This treaty had been negotiated in the 1920s as part of France's determination to surround Germany with a group of countries friendly to France and antagonistic to Germany.

I read to him [the Czech envoy] the key passages of the British memorandum of 22 May. The British government was not willing to support France in the Sudeten affair. . .

The Czechoslovak government must fully understand our position: France will not go to war for the Sudeten affair. Certainly, publicly we will affirm our solidarity, as the Czechoslovak government desires – but this affirmation of solidarity is to allow the Czechoslovak government to reach a peaceful and honourable solution. In no case must the Czechoslovak government think that if war breaks out we will be at her side. . .

(*Source:* Bonnet, French Foreign Minister, 20 July 1938: note of conversation with Czech envoy)

THINGS TO DO AND THINK ABOUT:

Compare Hitler's instructions to the Wehrmacht with the information given in the Hossbach memorandum (page 33). What, if anything, has changed?

Can you think of any explanations for this?

What explanation does Bonnet give for not honouring French treaty obligations to Czechoslovakia?

THE MUNICH CONFERENCE

Since Chamberlain was convinced that the Sudetenland would have to go to Germany, he embarked energetically on ensuring that war was avoided and that Hitler would negotiate a solution to the problem, rather than just seize the land.

A number of meetings were held and eventually, on 29 September, at a meeting between Britain, France, Germany and Italy, an agreement was signed which granted the Sudetenland to Germany. The Czechoslovak government was informed of the terms of the agreement after the meeting. Then Britain and Germany signed a statement agreeing that they would never go to war. Chamberlain returned home to a tumultuous reception, declaring "Peace in Our Time".

BRITISH REACTIONS TO MUNICH

The Daily Express, 30 September 1938:

PEACE

Be Glad in your hearts. Give thanks to your God.

The wings of peace settle about us and the peoples of Europe. The prayers of the troubled hearts are answered.
People of Britain, your children are safe.
Your husbands and your sons will not march to battle.
A war which would have been the most criminal, the most futile, the most destructive that ever insulted the purposes of men has been averted.
It was the war that nobody wanted.
Nobody in Germany. Nobody in France.
Nobody, above all, in Britain, which had no concern whatever with the issues at stake.
To him the laurels!
If we must have a victor, let us choose Chamberlain. For the prime minister's conquests are mighty and enduring – millions of happy homes and hearts relieved of their burden. To him the laurels!

hamberlain on his return from Munich, 30 September 1938. How liable is such a picture as measure of the popularity of Chamberlain's policy?

Winston Churchill to the House of Commons, 5 October 1938:

All is over. . . . Czechoslovakia recedes into the darkness. She has suffered in every respect by her association with the Western democracies. . . . She has suffered in particular from her association with France. . . . I think you will find that in a period of time which may be measured by years, but may be measured only by months, Czechoslovakia will be engulfed in the Nazi regime. . . . We are in the presence of a disaster of the first magnitude which has befallen Great Britain and France.

APPEASEMENT

Chamberlain's policy towards Hitler's claims is known as "Appeasement". Appeasement never meant peace at any price. The policy as it was applied by Conservative politicians who controlled the government of Britain in the 1930s, was seen as a realistic response to Germany's growing strength when Britain was relatively weak economically and in arms. The aim of the policy was to prevent Hitler from becoming over-dominant on mainland Europe. Since people generally felt revulsion at the thought of another war, the policy of appeasement had a real appeal and a lot of support among the British public.

The difficulty with such a policy rested in Chamberlain's (and his predecessors') assumption that Hitler wished, like them, to avoid war and that he accepted negotiation and agreed concessions as a proper way to conduct international affairs. He did not. In March 1939 German troops invaded Czechoslovakia.

THINGS TO DO AND THINK ABOUT:

Imagine that you are an adult negotiating with a child over the amount b which its pocket money should be increased. The child has, in your opinior a legitimate complaint that compared with what is given to other childre the pocket money is low. You agree with this. The child also argues tha increasing costs and wider interests mean that more pocket money i needed. All this you see as reasonable. An agreement is reached that, i exchange for the increase claimed, no further increase will be discussed fo a year. Everyone accepts the outcome. That is appeasement in practice.

PROBLEM: The child steals extra pocket money from your purse Negotiations are re-opened and a further increase is agreed, as the theft i seen as evidence that the first agreement was not for a large enoug increase.

PROBLEM: The child steals more money. What do you do now? Shoul you have done something different in the first place?

What are the advantages and disadvantages of drawing these sorts o parallels?

German troops enter Prague, March 1939. How accurate an idea of the Czech people's attitude to the German occupation can this picture give us? Is it a reliable piece of evidence?

Europe at War, 1939-41

Look back at the map of Europe on page 36. Hitler's occupation of Czechoslovakia had begun his eastern expansion. To the north of Czechoslovakia lay Poland, a country which everyone knew would be the next target for Hitler's expansion. Poland was a proud and nationalistic country whose existence had always been threatened (and often overcome) by one of her two powerful neighbours – Russia (now the Soviet Union) and Germany. The Treaty of Versailles had re-created Poland out of German and Soviet territory and given her a corridor to the sea. There was no way that she would yield up her new-found and precious national independence to the German state.

A Treaty of Friendship with Germany, signed in 1934, had been sufficient to maintain calm until 1939. Now Hitler made explicit his demands. He wanted a German corridor across the Polish corridor, to link Germany with East Prussia; the handing back to Germany of the international port of Danzig; and Poland's signature on the Anti-Comintern Pact, an agreement which bound Germany, Italy and Japan in enmity to the Soviet Union. From the beginning, Poland refused to make any concessions to German demands. To enter the Anti-Comintern Pact would be to invite retribution from her other neighbour. To concede on the corridor would be toinvite further demands from Hitler. The Western democracies tried to persuade Poland to compromise, but she refused to do so. Poland's determination to fight meant that war would certainly follow:

Hitler's attitude to Poland:

With minor exceptions German national unification has been achieved. Further successes cannot be achieved without bloodshed.

Poland will always be on the side of our adversaries. Despite the friendship agreement Poland has always intended to exploit every opportunity against us.

Danzig is not the objective. It is a matter of expanding our living space in the east, of making our food supplies secure, and of solving the problems of the Baltic states. To provide sufficient food you must have sparsely settled areas. This is fertile soil, whose surpluses will be very much increased by German, thorough management.

No other possibility can be seen in Europe. . . . There is therefore no question of sparing Poland, and the decision remains to attack Poland at the first suitable opportunity. . .

(*Source:* Hitler to the Generals, 23 May 1939, quoted in *Documents on German Foreign Policy 1919-1945)*

Does anything in the statement surprise you? Have Hitler's ideas changed?

Britain's attitude to Poland:

In order to make perfectly clear the position of His Majesty's Government

. . .I now have to inform the House that . . . in the event of any action which clearly threatened Polish independence, and which the Polish government accordingly considered it vital to resist with their national forces, His Majesty's government would feel themselves bound at once to lend the Polish government all support in their power. They have given the Polish government an assurance to this effect. The French government have authorized me to make plain that they stand in the same position.

(*Source:* Chamberlain to House of Commons, 31 March 1939)

Does anything in this statement surprise you? Have Chamberlain's idea. changed?

The attitude of France to Poland:

. . .Considering our situation was it better to be loyal to our commitments and go to war at once, or reconsider our position and profit from the respite obtained by increasing our military power, it being understood, that France ran the risk of being attacked in her turn after a delay of perhaps only a few months? . . .

In the course of several exchanges of opinion it was observed that even if we would be stronger in a few months Germany would also be much more so because she would dispose of Polish and Rumanian resources. Consequently France had no choice: the only solution possible was to keep our engagements towards Poland. . .

(*Source:* Minutes of meeting at French War Ministry, 23 August 1939)

THINGS TO DO AND THINK ABOUT:

Make a list of reasons that might have led Chamberlain to offer Poland one-sided guarantee.

Was war now more likely *or* inevitable*? Do you think Chamberlain saw it a* more likely *or* inevitable*?*

POLAND AND THE SOVIET UNION

In the eyes of many socialists in Western Europe, the Soviet Union was th only country to have attempted to take a stand against Hitler. The Sovie Union intervened actively on the side of the Republican government in th years of the Spanish Civil War, while the Western democracies had stoc by. She had offered to support the French guarantee of Czechoslovaki only to be brushed aside. She was the subject of vicious and vitriolic attack by Hitler, who saw communism as second only to Judaism as the sourc of all evil. With Soviet support, communists had stood shoulder to should with others in domestic struggles against fascism, for instance, in the Ea End of London when the British fascists tried to march through Jewis streets. It seemed to many that the only way to guarantee Polish securit

RENDEZVOUS

What do the insults in this cartoon of 20 September 1939 mean?

security, without a war, was to forge an alliance between Britain, France and the Soviet Union. This would surely deter even Hitler. Somewhat reluctantly, the British and French governments entered into negotiations with the Soviets on this question.

The news broke on 23 August that Germany and the Soviet Union had signed a non-aggression pact. It was greeted by many with disbelief and horror. When it became clear, a month later, that part of the deal had been Soviet occupation of half of Poland, outrage was added to bitterness.

A modern historian's view of the pact:

It is reasonable to assume that [Soviet interests] were twofold: to keep out of a European war, especially when they were actually engaged in serious fighting with the Japanese in the Far East . . . and to secure territory . . . which would add to Soviet security, internal as well as external. . . . The British and French offered nothing substantial under either heading. An alliance with them MIGHT deter Germany from going to war, but if it did not it would certainly involve the Soviet Union in conflict at once. The British were not prepared to pay the price for this risk and accept that the band of states from Finland to Rumania should become a Soviet sphere of influence. . . . The Germans on the other hand were able to meet both

Soviet interests. Instead of risk of war, they could offer certain neutrality. In terms of territory . . . they came bearing gifts, ready to carve up Poland. . .

Between the two sides the Soviet choice could scarcely be in doubt. It is only surprising that so much obloquy has been heaped on Stalin's head for making the best deal he could get. . .

(*Source:* P.M.H. Bell, *The Origins of the Second World War in Europe*, Longman, 1986)

THINGS TO DO AND THINK ABOUT:

What is Bell suggesting was motivating the Soviet Union's decisions? How are those motives different from or similar to those of France and Britain?

Was it principle *or* pragmatism *that was dictating Britain's foreign policy at this time? Do you think foreign policies should be based on* principles*?*

WAR IN TWO STAGES

Now that Hitler could be sure that no threat would come from the East, he could risk a declaration of war from the West. Without the Soviet Union there would be little the French and British could do in reality, to prevent a German conquest of Poland. So, on 1 September 1939, German troops invaded Poland. For some time it was not clear whether Britain and France would stand by their guarantees, but finally, on 3 September 1939, Britain and then France declared that a state of war existed between themselves and Germany.

Poland fell within a matter of weeks. In the spring of 1940 Germany successfully invaded Western Europe. By June 1940 only Britain and her empire remained at war against Hitler.

Encouraged by the enormous military successes of the German armed forces in Poland and the West, and convinced that he had the beating of any army, Hitler set in motion the search for living space, the search for resources, and the elimination of "sub-species" such as Slavs and Jews which he had described in his book and his memoranda.

DIRECTIVE 21

The German armed forces must be prepared, even before the conclusion of the war against England, to crush Soviet Russia in a rapid campaign.

. . .I shall issue orders for the deployment against Soviet Russia eight weeks before the operation is timed to begin. Preparations that require more time than this will be put in hand now and will be concluded by 15 May 1941.

It is of decisive importance that our intention to attack should not be known.

(*Source:* Directive from Hitler to German Armed Forces, 18 December 1940, quoted in Shuter and Lewis, *Skills in History*, Heinemann, 1988)

On 22 June 1941 Operation Barbarossa, the code name for the attack on the Soviet Union, was launched. In this action Hitler opened up the possibility of his eventual defeat.

THINGS TO DO AND THINK ABOUT:

Why was it important that the intention to attack should be kept secret?

Into War: The Far East, 1937-41

While Germany was testing the resolve and strength of Britain and Franc[e] through her expansionist foreign policy in Europe, Japan embarked on [a] course which would ultimately bring her into conflict with both th[e] European colonial powers (Britain, France and the Netherlands) and th[e] USA. As we have seen (pages 25-27), pressures inside Japan had led to th[e] growth and popularity of right-wing nationalist forces, and particularly th[e] army. Success in Manchuria had raised Japanese self-esteem an[d] increasingly it was seen as important to maintain and, if possible, exten[d] Japanese rights through the rest of China.

In China itself, the nationalist government was becoming stronger an[d] more respected as it first extended its control over areas previousl[y] dominated by war-lords and then mounted a fierce attack on the Chines[e] communists and drove them out of their urban strongholds into the Lon[g] March for survival. By 1937 the nationalist government under Chiang Kai[-] shek was internationally recognized as the sole representative of China'[s] interests.

FIGHTING ON THE MARCO POLO BRIDGE

A strong and independent China was not something the governments o[f] Japan could allow to develop. As long as China was torn by civil war, relian[t] on Japanese support, her independence was assured; but as th[e] nationalist government, based at Nanking, gained strength, so the pressur[e] grew on the Japanese to weaken that government and secure Japan's ow[n] power in China.

From *The Times* China correspondent, 9 July 1937:

FIGHTING NEAR PEKING
MANY CASUALTIES

Peking July [8]

Martial Law has been declared in Peking as a result of serious fighting this morning between Chinese and Japanese troops near Wangping, a small walled town 30 miles west of the city. . . . The Chinese lay the blame for the situation on the widespread Japanese field exercises which have been proceeding during the last few days. The trouble seems to have started when Chinese troops mistook a sham attack on Marco Polo bridge near Wangping for a real one.

Nanking July 8 – The Chinese Foreign Office has protested to the Japanese Embassy here against the 'provocative activities of the Japanese forces in North China'.

From *The Times* Japan correspondent, 9 July 1937:

Tokyo July 8 – The Japanese third fleet has been instructed to stand by. It is reported from Peking that the negotiations there have so far proved fruitless and the Chinese authorities are accused of showing a 'total lack of sincerity'.

***The Times* leader, 14 July 1937:**

Warfare, though not yet war, now rages at the gates of that pleasant city [Peking]. . . . Appropriately terrible words are uttered by the two governments concerned. . . . Beyond the western suburbs of Peking rifles and machine guns wrangle with a growing intolerance.
Why? Nobody really knows. . . .
While the Japanese Army may go to extremes in the field the Japanese government is fully alive to the perils of adventure. . . . To declare war, to seize Peking . . . Japan would find such action easy and . . . enjoyable. But none can believe that Japanese statesmanship . . . would entertain so desperate . . . a project. . .

THE CHINA INCIDENT

Possibly no one was quite sure how the first shots came to be fired in the "China Incident", as the Japanese called the eight-year undeclared war that followed the fight at Marco Polo bridge. But this event marked the start of Japanese involvement in a shooting war that was eventually to draw Japan and the United States into the war in Europe and turn that into a truly world war. Once hostilities *had* broken out, the Japanese civilian government under Prince Konoye was reluctant to end them while military gains were being made which might secure Japanese interests in China.

THE NEW ORDER

The war was allowed to drift on. By the following autumn many important Chinese cities had fallen to the Japanese, but much of the great hinterland of China remained out of Japan's control. China's nationalist or Kuomintang government set up its headquarters at Chungking. The Chinese communists, who had survived their Long March and were now gathering strength in the stronghold at Yenan, embarked on a successful guerilla war behind the Japanese lines. In November 1938 the Japanese government in Tokyo issued this statement:

By the august virtue of His Majesty, our naval and military forces have captured Canton and the three cities of Wuhan; and all the vital areas of China have thus fallen into our hands. The Kuomintang Government exists no longer except as a mere local regime. However, so long as it persists in its anti-Japanese and pro-communist policy our country will not lay down its arms – never until that regime is crushed.

What Japan seeks is the establishment of a new order which will ensure the permanent stability of East Asia. In this lies the ultimate purpose of our present military campaign. . .

. . .Its object is to secure international justice, to perfect the joint defence against Communism, and to create a new culture and realize a close economic cohesion throughout East Asia. . .

The establishment of a new order in East Asia is in complete conformity with the very spirit in which the Empire was founded. To achieve such a task is the exalted responsibility with which our generation is entrusted. . .

(*Source:* Statement by Japanese government, 3 November 1938, quoted in Maki, *Conflict and Tension in the Far East – Key Documents 1894-1960*, University of Washington Press, 1961)

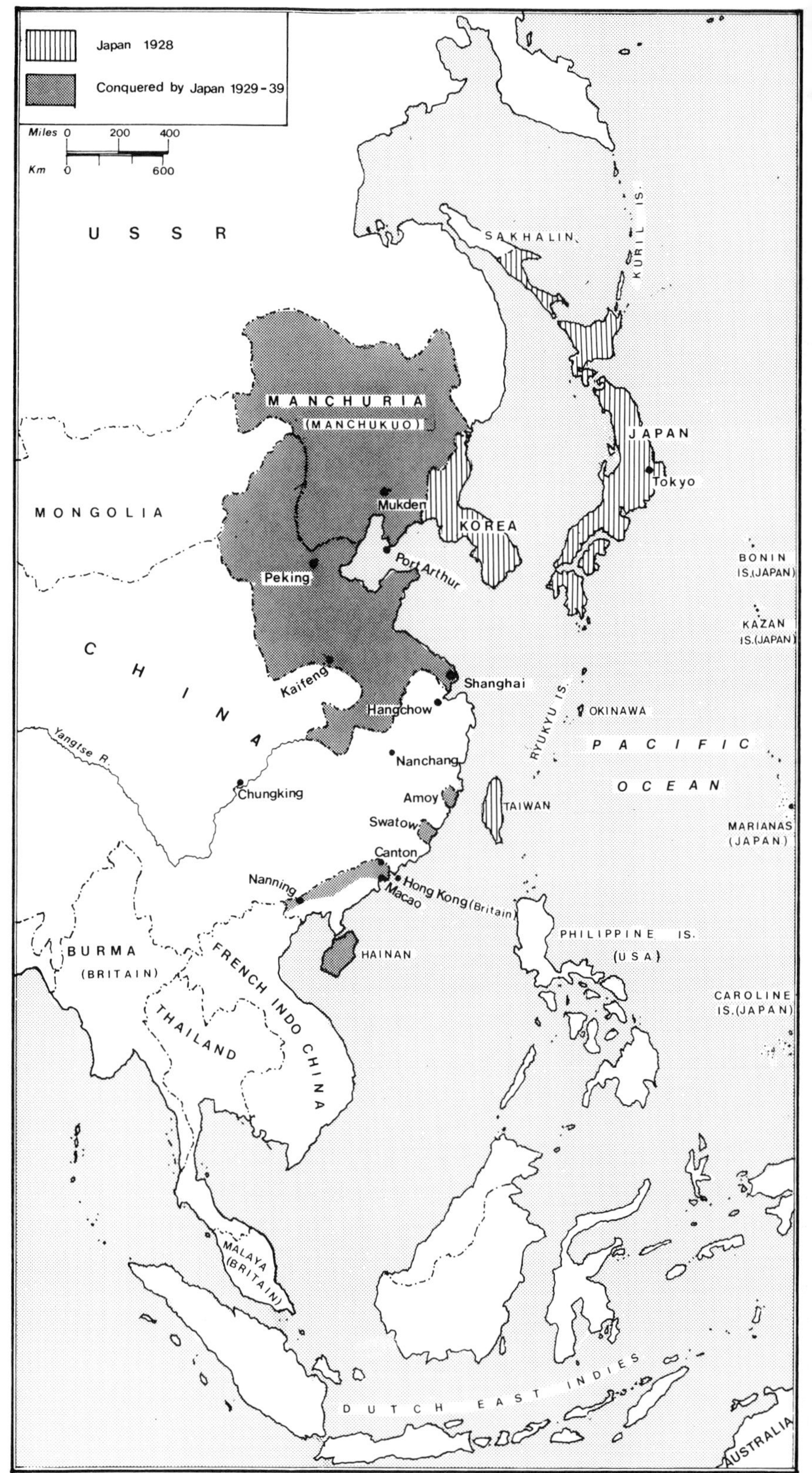
Japan 1928
Conquered by Japan 1929-39
Miles 0 200 400
Km 0 600
U S S R
SAKHALIN
KURIL IS.
MANCHURIA
(MANCHUKUO)
JAPAN
Tokyo
MONGOLIA
Mukden
KOREA
Peking
Port Arthur
BONIN IS.(JAPAN)
KAZAN IS.(JAPAN)
CHINA
Kaifeng
Shanghai
Hangchow
RYUKYU IS.
OKINAWA
Yangtse R.
PACIFIC
OCEAN
Nanchang
Chungking
Amoy
TAIWAN
Swatow
MARIANAS (JAPAN)
Canton
Nanning
Hong Kong (Britain)
Macao
PHILIPPINE IS.
(USA)
HAINAN
BURMA
(BRITAIN)
FRENCH INDO CHINA
THAILAND
CAROLINE IS.(JAPAN)
MALAYA (BRITAIN)
DUTCH EAST INDIES
AUSTRALIA

The expansion of the Japanese empire.

INTERNATIONAL SUPPORT FOR THE KUOMINTANG

Unfortunately for Japan, the Kuomintang government would not lie down and die, or accept the New Order. If you study the map carefully, you will see that the Japanese had not succeeded in cutting the nationalists off from the west. The nationalist government in Chungking was supported by supplies coming in through French Indo-China and along the Burma Road from British-held Burma. Further support for the Chinese came from the United States. Though neutral and still isolationist in outlook, the United States was viewing with concern Japanese power in the Pacific, long regarded as an area of particular American interest.

THINGS TO DO AND THINK ABOUT:

Study the New Order statement carefully. With what is the Emperor attributed? Why is the Japanese government putting so much emphasis on the communist threat? What do you think the Japanese government means by international justice?

WAR BREAKS OUT IN EUROPE: THE JAPANESE REACTION

The outbreak of war in Europe and the swift defeat of France in the spring of 1940 transformed the situation in the Far East. If you study the map on page 48, you will see that the European colonial powers in the Far East were Holland, Britain and France. Holland and France were now occupied by Japan's ally, Germany, and Britain stood alone, facing almost certain invasion. Seeing an opportunity to strengthen her position in the war with China, Japan demanded that France accept a Japanese mission in French Indo-China. The defeated French government agreed to this. Japan then threatened Britain with war if she did not close the Burma Road. In September 1940 the military mission in Indo-China was converted to a full-scale military occupation.

Japanese expansion:

On 4 September the Japanese government agreed a policy document which outlined the limits of the New Order:

Japan's sphere of living for the construction of a greater East Asia New Order will comprise: the former German islands under mandate, French Indochina and Pacific islands, Thailand, British Malaya, British Borneo, Dutch East Indies, Burma, Australia, New Zealand, India etc. with Japan, Manchuria and China as the backbone.

(*Source:* quoted in Parkinson, *Attack on Pearl Harbour*, Wayland, 1973)

Remember that Japan had been particularly badly hit by the American Depression. What were the economic advantages to her of extending the New Order to all these countries?

THE UNITED STATES' REACTION

The defeat of France and the predicament of Britain at last galvanized the United States into action. Three major policy decisions were made. First, a National Defence Act was passed in May 1940. It permitted the US President to ban the export of goods with military value, if he regarded such a ban as necessary for national defence. Then, in January 1941, a new set of US military plans was approved. These plans openly accepted the prospect of war both in the west and in the east. The overall plan (Plan Dog) proposed an American *offensive* war in the Atlantic, but a *defensive* war in the Pacific. Not even the Americans regarded it as possible to wage a war on two fronts. Finally, in March 1941, the United States Congress passed the Lend Lease Bill which allowed the President to supply the British war effort with loaned American war goods.

The President of the United States, F. D. Roosevelt, had been campaigning for some time for a greater American commitment to the Western democracies, as Britain and France were called. Here he justifies that view in a speech to the American people.

The British People are conducting an active war against the unholy alliance. . . . Our own future security is greatly dependent on that outcome. . . . I make the direct statement to the American people that there is far less chance of the United States getting into the war if we do all we can now to support the nations defending themselves against attack.

(*Source:* F. D. Roosevelt, 29 December 1940)

As part of her policy to try to prevent the situation in the Far East from turning into war, America imposed sanctions against the Japanese, following their occupation of Indo-China. For instance, she banned the export to Japan of iron and steel scrap and fuel – a ban which could have had a disastrous effect on Japan and her industry and military strength. Japan was also prevented from taking back anything that she owned in the United States, such as stocks and shares, industries or government bonds.

JAPANESE REACTIONS TO THE UNITED STATES

In September 1940 Japan, Germany and Italy signed the Tripartite Pact.

. . .the Governments of Germany, Italy and Japan have agreed as follows:
I. Japan recognizes and respects the leadership of Germany and Italy in the establishment of a new order in Europe.
II. Germany and Italy recognize and respect the leadership of Japan in the establishment of a new order in Greater East Asia.
III. Germany, Italy and Japan . . . undertake to assist one another with all political, economic and military means when one of the three contracting powers is attacked by a Power at present not involved in the European war or in the Chinese-Japanese conflict.

(*Source:* Mutual Assistance Pact, Berlin, 27 September 1940, quoted in Maki, *Conflict and Tension in the Far East – Key Documents 1894-1960*, University of Washington Press, 1961)

THINGS TO DO AND THINK ABOUT:

Why do you think Germany was eager to sign the Mutual Assistance Pact?

Why might the United States have seen holding off Japan as a way of helping Great Britain?

JAPAN DECIDES ON WAR

In April 1941 Japan signed a non-aggression pact with the Soviet Union. This successfully secured the northern frontier of Manchukuo, where sporadic, bitter and costly fighting against the Soviet Union had been going on since 1931. In June 1941, when Germany launched her attack on the Soviets, there was some pressure from the Japanese army and some temptation for Japan to break the non-aggression pact and thrust north into the Soviet Union. This would have been an easy war to win and would not have incurred the wrath of the United States. However, Japan resisted the temptation. The oil and rubber she needed, both for her industries and to bring the China Incident to a successful conclusion, lay to the south. The supply route for the Chungking government lay in the south. And the Japanese navy was convinced that it could deal a swift and deadly blow to the United States by attacking her fleet where it was anchored at Pearl Harbor, so America's enmity need not be feared.

NEGOTIATIONS CONTINUE

Nevertheless, if war could be avoided, both Japan and the United States would prefer to do so. They negotiated throughout 1941, in an attempt to find a way through the difficulties. America could not accept Japanese power extending throughout the Pacific; Japan could not accept America's right to restrain her pursuing policies necessary for her survival as a nation. Both sides recognized there was little chance for a successful resolution. The Americans wanted time in which to implement Plan Dog by strengthening their fleets on both seaboards as well as reinforcing their garrisons in the Philippines. For the Japanese, on the other hand, time was running out. Unless Japan could find access to oil and steel and rubber soon, her efforts in China and her own industries would fail.

Speed becomes essential:

On 5 November 1941, at a joint liaison conference in Tokyo between the Japanese government and the chiefs of staff, the problem facing Japan was put like this:

. . .since the probability of victory in the initial stages of the war is sufficiently high, I am convinced that we should take advantage of that assured victory and turn the heightened morale of the people, who are determined to overcome the national crisis even at the cost of their lives, toward production as well as toward [reduced] consumption and other aspects of national life. In terms of maintaining and augmenting our national strength, this would be better than just sitting tight and waiting for the enemy to put pressure on us.

(*Source:* Lt-Gen Suzuki Teiichi, President of the Planning Board for Resources, 5 November 1941, quoted in Maison and Caiger, *A History of Japan*, Cassell Australia, 1972)

A proposed agreement:

On 26 November 1941 the American government handed an outline of an agreement to the Japanese ambassador. It included the following proposed clauses:

3. The Government of Japan will withdraw all military, naval, air and police forces from China and from Indochina.
4. The Government of the United States and the Government of Japan will not support . . . any government . . . in China other than the National Government . . . with capital . . . at Chungking.
6. The Government of the United States and the Government of Japan will enter into negotiations for the conclusion . . . of a trade agreement . . . including an undertaking by the United States to bind raw silk on the free list.
7. The Government of the United States . . . will . . . remove the freezing restrictions on Japanese funds in the United States. . .

What is the United States offering Japan and in exchange for what? Do you think it likely that the Japanese would have found such terms acceptable? Why?

THE JAPANESE

The Japanese reply was twofold. In Washington, the Japanese ambassador, Nomura, handed a Memorandum to the US Secretary of State, Cordell Hull, on 7 December 1941.

. . .
4. It is impossible not to reach the conclusion that the American Government desires to maintain and strengthen, in coalition with Great Britain and other powers, its dominant position. . . . It is a fact of history that the countries of East Asia for the past hundred years or more have been compelled to observe the status quo under the Anglo-American policy of imperialistic exploitation. . .
5. In brief, the American proposal contains certain acceptable items such as those concerning commerce, including the conclusions of a trade agreement. . . . On the other hand, however, the proposal in question ignores Japan's sacrifices in the four years of the China Affair, menaces the Empire's existence itself and disparages its honour and prestige. . .
7. Obviously it is the intention of the American Government to conspire with Great Britain . . . to obstruct Japan's efforts towards the establishment of peace through the creation of a new order in East Asia. . .
The Japanese Government regrets to have to notify hereby the American Government that in view of the attitude of the American Government it

cannot but consider that it is impossible to reach an agreement through further negotiation.

While Hull was reading this Memorandum, the Japanese navy and airforce delivered Japan's other reply in Pearl Harbor.

WORLD WAR DECLARED

A formal declaration of war, by the Japanese, against Britain and the United States, was read to the Japanese people. The following day a delighted Britain and the United States declared war on Japan. On 11 December, Germany and Italy kept to the terms of the Tripartite Pact and declared war on the United States. Hitler was pleased that his silent enemy, the United States, was at last at open war.

VICTORY IN SIGHT

Winston Churchill, now Prime Minister of Britain, described his feelings at America's entry into the war:

So we had won after all! Yes, after Dunkirk; after the fall of France . . . after the threat of invasion. . . . We had won the war. England would live; Britain would live; the Commonwealth of Nations and the Empire would live. How long the war would last or in what fashion it would end no man could tell, nor did I at this moment care . . . we should emerge . . . safe and victorious.

(*Source:* Winston Churchill in *The Second World War, Vol. III: The Grand Alliance*, Cassell, 1950)

THINGS TO DO AND THINK ABOUT:

From all you have read, can you list the enabling causes that brought war to the Far East?

The Japanese attack on Pearl Harbor. The US battleship California *settles into the mud. What effect would photographs such as this have had on domestic American opinion?*

Epilogue

So, in December 1941, the whole intricate series of events which we have been studying came together to create the final event – the Second World War. And yet that event was not in itself final, for in its shaping were rooted the causes that would produce the Allies' victory.

Hitler's invasion of the Soviet Union faltered before the gates of Moscow, and ended at the siege of Stalingrad. Germany was equipped to fight a series of short wars; once the long, slow war of the Russian winter and the Russian army took hold, Germany had difficulty sustaining her resources.

THE RUSSIAN ARMY

The advance of a Russian Army is something that Westerners can't imagine. Behind the tank spearheads rolls on a vast horde, largely mounted on horses. The soldier carries a sack on his back, with dry crusts of bread and raw vegetables collected on the march from the fields and villages. The horses eat the straw from the house roofs – they get very little else. The Russians are accustomed to carry on for as long as three weeks in this primitive way, when advancing. You can't stop them like an ordinary army. . .

(*Source:* A.V. Karasay, *The Great Patriotic War*, quoted in Purnell's *History of the Twentieth Century* no. 69)

The Soviet army advanced to Berlin, a city now utterly devastated by the effects of bombing and the war.

American troops raising the flag at Iwo Jima. This image of the war was used as the model for the American war memorial in Washington DC.

THE UNITED STATES The enormous economic strength of the United States meant that, contrary to all her plans, she did in fact succeed in fighting a war simultaneously in Europe and in the Pacific.

DEATH But the real epilogue to war is death.

Nagasaki

Dazed I retreated into the consulting room, in which the only upright object on the rubbish-strewn floor was my desk. I went and sat on it and looked out of the window. . . . Gradually the veiled ground became visible, and the view beyond rooted me to the spot with horror.

All the buildings I could see were on fire: large ones and small ones and those with straw-thatched roofs. . . . Trees on the nearby hills were smoking, as were the leaves of sweet potatoes in the fields. It seemed as if

Hiroshima, 6 August 1945.

the earth itself emitted fire and smoke, flames that writhed up and erupted from underground. . . . It seemed like the end of the world.

(*Source:* Tatsichiro Akizzuki, *Nagasaki 1945*, Quartet, 1981)

Estimates of war dead among the major combatants:

USSR	20,000,000
Germany and Austria	6,500,000
Poland	6,000,000
Japan	1,900,000
France	600,000
Italy	400,000
Britain	390,000
USA	300,000

These figures include military and civilian deaths. No estimate is made of the numbers of wounded, homeless, dispossessed. It is worth remembering that the Second World War was the first war to produce more civilian than military casualties. Altogether, some 45 million people died, 6 million of them Jews.

Refugee blues:

This poem was written in March 1939

Say this city had ten million souls
Some are living in mansions, some are living in holes:
Yet there's no place for us, my dear, yet there's no place for us.

Once we had a country and we thought it fair,
Look in the atlas and you'll find it there:
We cannot go there now, my dear, we cannot go there now.

Belsen. It was not until the news reporters and photographers entered the death camps with the advancing armies that the full horror of the Nazi Reich came home to people.

In the village churchyard there grows an old yew,
Every spring it blossoms anew:
Old passports can't do that my dear, old passports can't do that.

The consul banged the table and said;
'If you've got no passport you're officially dead':
But we are still alive my dear, but we are still alive.

Went to a committee; they offered me a chair;
Asked me politely to return next year:
But where shall we go today, my dear, but where shall we go today?

Came to a public meeting; the speaker got up and said:
'If we let them in, they will steal our daily bread';
He was talking of you and me, my dear, he was talking of you and me.

Thought I heard the thunder rumbling in the sky;
It was Hitler over Europe, saying: 'They must die';
O we were in his mind, my dear, O we were in his mind.

Saw a poodle in a jacket fastened with a pin,
Saw a door opened and a cat let in:
But they weren't German Jews, my dear, but they weren't German Jews.

Went down the harbour and stood upon the quay,
Saw the fish swimming as if they were free:
Only ten feet away, my dear, only ten feet away.

Walked through a wood, saw the birds in the trees;
They had no politicians and sang at their ease:
They weren't the human race, my dear, they weren't the human race.

Dreamed I saw a building with a thousand floors,
A thousand windows and a thousand doors;
Not one of them was ours my dear, not one of them was ours.

Stood on a great plain in the falling snow;
Ten thousand soldiers marched to and fro:
Looking for you and me, my dear, looking for you and me.

(*Source:* W.H. Auden, *Collected Poems of W.H. Auden*, Faber, 1976)

THINGS TO DO AND THINK ABOUT:

Was the Second World War a just war?

Sources

Extensive sources are now available both on the war itself and on the period leading up to its outbreak. However the sources available in this country and in English tend to be almost exclusively about the *European* war. There is little easily available source – material on the Japanese/Pacific war, and much of what can be found needs to be approached very carefully as it tends to be racist and polemical. Similar care needs to be taken with memoirs of the European war. When the consequences of one's actions include the deaths of millions, it is hard not to be self-justificatory in one's writing about what happened.

Collections of documents

Documents on German Foreign Policy 1919-1945 and *Documents on British Foreign Policy 1919-1939* are both published by HMSO. The texts of treaties can be found in J.A.S. Grenville, *The Major International Treaties, 1914-1973* (London, 1974). For Japan, the best collection is John M. Maki, *Conflict and Tension in the Far East – Key Documents 1894-1960* (University of Washington Press, 1961). These are all fairly heavy-going, however, and it is becoming increasingly easy to find edited collections of sources, although these must obviously be used with care. A good general source of documents for the European War is Anthony P. Adamthwaite, *The Making of the Second World War* (London, 1979).

Memoirs and other personal sources

Again, there are many of these; the following is only a selection: David Dilks (ed.), *The Diaries of Sir Alexander Cadogan, 1938-1945* (London, 1971) (Cadogan was Permanent Under Secretary at the Foreign Office during those years); Adolf Hitler, *Mein Kampf* (tr. by D.C. Watt), (London, 1974); Cordell Hull, *Memoirs*, (London, 1959) (Cordell Hull was the American Cabinet member dealing with Foreign Affairs); Roosevelt Elliot (ed.), *FDR – His Personal Letters* (New York, 1950).

Newspapers and cartoons

Although most of us can look only at British ones, these can nevertheless help us to have a different view of events from the more official versions we read. Most reference libraries stock at least one national newspaper and a local one too. Look for comments on Munich and the *Anschluss*.

Britain

Alternative perceptions of the same events are to be found in Keith Feiling, *The Life of Neville Chamberlain* (London, 1946) and Winston Churchill, *The Second World War vol. 1 The Gathering Storm* (London, 1948). A detailed study of the apparent turning point in appeasement is offered in Simon Newman, *March 1939 The British Guarantee to Poland* (Oxford, 1976), and William R. Rock, *British Appeasement in the 1930s* (London, 1977) is a fairly vigorous attack on Chamberlain's policies.

Germany

The classic work on Hitler is Alan Bullock, *Hitler. A study in tyranny* (Harmondsworth, 1962) and a closer look at the foreign policy of this period is to be found in William Carr, *Arms, Autarky and Aggression. A study in German Foreign Policy, 1933-1939* (London, 1972).

The United States

Two special studies of the period are Langer and Gleason, *The Challenge to Isolation 1937-1940* (New York, 1952) and John E. Wiltz, *From Isolation to War 1933-1941* (London, 1968).

Japan

A detailed study of the debates within Japan leading up to the attack on Pearl Harbor are to be found in Ike, *Japan's Decision for War – Records of the 1941 Policy Conferences* (Stanford University Press, 1967). A rare look at the Japanese perspective in these years is Tsuji, *Singapore – the Japanese Version* (trans. M.E. Lake) (Sydney, 1960). It is worth trying to understand more about Japanese society and history and a good general history is Mason and Caiger, *A History of Japan* (Cassell Australia, 1972).

General Works

The classic book is A.J.P. Taylor, *The Origins of the Second World War* (London, 1961), which is both entertaining and provocative. A good look at the ensuing debates is to be found in W. Roger Louis (ed.), *The Origins of the Second World War. A.J.P. Taylor and his critics* (New York, 1970). There is also P.M.H. Bell, *The Origins of the Second World War in Europe* (Longman, 1986).

Biographies

CHAMBERLAIN, Neville (1869-1940)
Chamberlain was a member of a famous political family. His father, Joseph Chamberlain, had been a colourful and powerful politician around the turn of the century, and his brother, Austin, a close associate of Lloyd George. Neville Chamberlain became an MP after the First World War. During the 1930s he became Chancellor of the Exchequer and was a highly regarded member of Baldwin's cabinet. On becoming Prime Minister, in 1937, he pursued an active foreign policy, based on the assumption, which had been shared by previous governments, that all civilized peoples would wish to avoid war; therefore, sensible compromises could and should be made. This policy was known as appeasement. When Hitler invaded Western Europe in the spring of 1940, Chamberlain's previous policies led the Conservatives to feel that he would not prosecute the war vigorously enough. He was replaced as Prime Minister by Winston Churchill, and died soon afterwards.

CHURCHILL Winston Spencer (1874-1965)
Churchill was born in Blenheim Palace, Oxfordshire, the home of his grandfather, the Duke of Marlborough. He entered Parliament as a Unionist (Conservative) in 1900, but that party's proposals for tariff reform in 1903 drove him into the Liberal Party. The Conservatives almost never forgave him for this, as they place a very high premium on party loyalty. In 1924, he rejoined the Conservative Party and became Chancellor of the Exchequer. When Chamberlain became Prime Minister in 1937, Churchill – no longer in the government – began a sustained attack on the policy of appeasement. On the outbreak of war he was brought back into the cabinet as First Lord of the Admiralty, a post he had held in the First World War, under Lloyd George. In May 1940, as German troops swept through Western Europe, he became Prime Minister, a post he held throughout the war.

HITLER Adolf (1889-1945)
Leader of Germany, 1933-45. He grew up in poverty in Austria. When war broke out in 1914 he joined the German army, was promoted to Corporal and won the Iron Cross, a medal for bravery. After the First World War he founded the Nazi Party, to restore German greatness by overthrowing the Treaty of Versailles, finding "living space" for the German people, and getting rid of Jews, whom he saw, along with Marxists, as responsible for Germany's problems. He was a first-class propagandist and this, combined with wealthy support and the Great Depression, helped him to win power in Germany in 1933. He embarked upon a rule of domestic terror, huge government spending (which reduced unemployment), massive re-armament and an expansionist foreign policy which led to the Second World War. Although initially successful, his invasion of the Soviet Union ensured Germany's eventual defeat. Hitler killed himself in April 1945, as the Red Army entered Berlin's suburbs.

KONOYE Fumimaro (1891-1945)
Konoye became Prime Minister of Japan on 3 June 1937, a month before the "China Incident". He was a prince of illustrious Fujiwara ancestry and close to the throne. Some Japanese leaders hoped that he would be able to control the growing influence of the military. Though Konoye did manage to keep the initiative in the hands of the civilian members of his government, the fighting in China ensured increasing power for the military. By the time Konoye became Prime Minister for the second time in July 1940, the conditions for Japan's southward expansion had been laid. He resigned finally in October 1941 over the question of continuing negotiations with the United States, and was replaced by General Hideki TOJO, whose military career and decisive character (in contrast to Konoye's non-belligerent approach) give a suggestion of drastic change which is probably misleading.

MUSSOLINI Benito (1883-1945)
Mussolini was the son of a blacksmith and a school teacher. Before the First World War he was an ardent socialist and worked for a time as a school teacher and then a journalist. He served as a soldier in the war and afterwards founded the Italian Fascist Party. Its main policy was Action. Italian politics after the war were very unstable and it was hard for the democratic governments to pursue clear and consistent policies. In 1922 Mussolini led his party in a march on Rome and was asked by the King to form a government. From then on the Fascist Party took control of more and more of the state machine and Mussolini became the Italian dictator, although Italy remained a monarchy. In the 1930s Italian

oreign policy became ncreasingly aggressive and Italy Irew closer to Germany, but it vas not until 1940 that Mussolini ook Italy into the Second World Var. On 10 July 1943 the Allies nvaded Sicily and on 25 July Mussolini fell from power. In April 945 the war in Italy ended and n 29 April Italian Partisans, who ad been fighting the Germans in he mountains, found Mussolini rying to escape. He was shot.

ROOSEVELT Franklin Delano (1882-1945)

Roosevelt was first elected President of the United States in 932. He was re-elected four mes. He was born at Hyde Park, n New York State, and was the on of a wealthy landowner. In 921 he caught polio and was paralysed from the waist down, but he taught himself to walk again, with the aid of crutches. As the European dictatorships grew stronger, Roosevelt tried to persuade the American people to take a more active role in European affairs, but it was not until war actually broke out in Europe that the American Congress was prepared to pass legislation to enable Roosevelt to help the British war effort. In August 1941 he met Winston Churchill at sea and drew up the Atlantic Charter which defined the war aims of the Allies. He died in office in April 1945, before the war ended.

STALIN Josef (1879-1953)

Stalin was born in Georgia, a province of Russia. His mother was washerwoman and his father a shoemaker. He became a socialist and began to work to get rid of the Tsarist government of Russia. In 1905, he became a supporter of Lenin, who was to lead the successful Revolution in 1971. After Lenin's death in 1924 Stalin, who was General Secretary of the Communist Party, became increasingly powerful. During the 1930s he organized the trial and execution of many of his old contemporaries and millions of ordinary Soviet people were imprisoned or sent to the labour camps. In 1939 Stalin and Hitler signed a non-aggression pact, which kept the Soviet Union out of the war until June 1941, when the German army invaded. Stalin died in 1953.

Glossary

Allies military alliance of which Britain was a part
arsenal collection of arms/arms store
Blitzkrieg lightning war
Chancellor head of the German government
Christian Pacifist someone who rejects war on the basis of the teachings of Christ
Comintern the Communist International led by the Soviet Union
contracting parties individuals or groups signing an agreement
coupons used in rationing, a system for regulating the issue of clothes and food
Cpl. Corporal
edema a medical condition of which one symptom may be swelling of the ankles or other joints
evacuated removed from danger
fascism a political ideology glorifying the power of the state
field exercises practising war, for soldiers
free list list of goods which may be admitted to a country free of tariff or charge
Geneva headquarters of the League of Nations
Centre of Disarmament Conference
Good Housekeeping a magazine
hurricane British fighter aircraft
Kuomintang Chinese Nationalist Party
legitimate allowable, permitted
Marks German units of currency
Meiji (1) Emperor Meiji, who came to the throne in 1868; (2) also used to describe the period following the changes in the constitution and domestic and foreign policy which brought Japan to world power status by 1920
octane fuel
plate false teeth
plebiscite referendum
ratification confirmation of treaty. The US constitution requires the Senate to agree to (ratify) any treaty signed by the President by a two-thirds majority
Reich empire
reparations sums of money to be paid in compensation for damage and suffering caused in war
rescript an official text
Sgt. sergeant
shrapnel small pieces of metal released from an exploding shell
spitfire British fighter aircraft
Sudetendeutsche German-speaking people living in the Sudetenland (part of Czechoslovakia)
Transvaal a province of the Union of South Africa
tyranny unfettered power
Uitlanders English-speaking people living in the Transvaal before the Boer War
volte-face about face

Date List

1919	Jan-June: Paris Peace Conference.
	June: Versailles Treaty.
	Nazi Party established.
1920	League of Nations established.
	Jan: USA votes against Versailles Treaty and the League.
	German reparations fixed at £6,600 million.
1922	Washington Naval Conference limits size of Japanese navy.
	Oct: Mussolini marches on Rome.
1923	Feb: France occupies Ruhr.
	German economy collapses.
	Sept: Great Tokyo earthquake; more than 100,000 dead.
1924	Sept: Dawes Plan.
1925	Dec: Treaty of Locarno.
1926	Dec: Hirohito Emperor of Japan.
1929	Oct: Wall Street Crash.
1930	Sept: Nazi gains in German elections.
1931	Sept: Japan invades Manchuria.
1933	March: Nazis come to power in Germany.
	Hitler Chancellor.
	Germany withdraws from League of Nations.
1935	German re-armament.
1936	March: Germany occupies Rhineland.
	August: Compulsory military service in Germany.
1937	July: Japanese invasion of China.
1938	Feb: Hitler commander of armed services.
	Mar: *Anschluss*.
	Sept: Munich Conference.
	Annexation of Sudetenland by Germany.
1939	March: Germany invades rest of Czechoslovakia.
	Aug: Nazi/Soviet pact.
	Sept: Germany invades Poland.
	Sept: France and Britain declare war on Germany.
1940	May: Churchill Prime Minister of Great Britain.
	June: Fall of France.
	Italy enters war on Germany's side.
1941	March: Lend Lease Act passed.
	June: Germany invades Soviet Union.
	Dec: Pearl Harbor: Japan and USA enter war.
1945	May: Germany surrenders.
	August: Hiroshima and Nagasaki bomb.
	Sept: Japan surrenders.

Index

Rosie's Babies

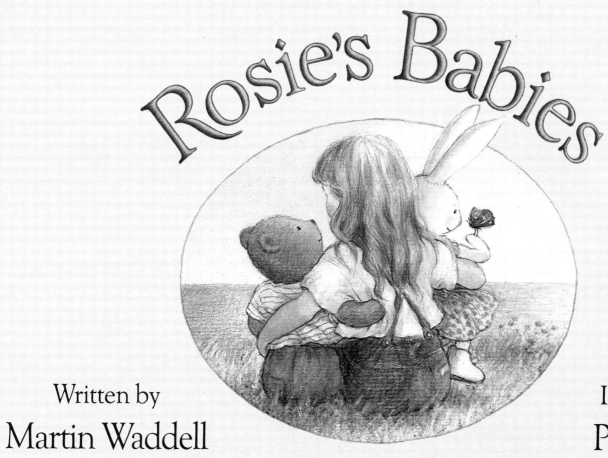

Written by
Martin Waddell

Illustrated by
Penny Dale

WALKER BOOKS
LONDON

Mum was putting the baby to bed and Rosie said, "I've got two babies and you've only got one."

"Two, including you," said Mum.

"I'm not a baby, I'm four years old," said Rosie.

"Tell me about your babies," Mum said.

And Rosie said,
"My babies live in a bird's nest and they are nearly as big as me. They go out in the garden all by themselves and sometimes they make me cross!"
"Do they?" said Mum.
"Yes, when they do silly things!" said Rosie.
"What silly things do they do?" asked Mum.

And Rosie said,
"My babies climbed a big mountain. That was silly, because they couldn't get down. They jumped, and they bumped on their bottoms!"
"Silly babies," said Mum.
"Did they hurt themselves?"

And Rosie said,
"One of my babies hurt her knee.
I bandaged it up and she cried
and I said 'Never mind'
because I am kind."
"I'm sure you are," said Mum.
"What else do your babies do?"

And Rosie said,
"My babies drive cars that are real ones and lorries and dumpers and boats. My babies are very good drivers."
"What do your babies like doing best?" asked Mum.

And Rosie said,
"My babies like swings and rockers and dinosaurs. They go to the park when it's dark and there are no mums and dads who can see, only me!"
"Gracious!" said Mum.
"Aren't they scared?"

And Rosie said,
"My babies are scared of the big dogs, but I'm not. I go GRRRRRRRRRRRRR! and frighten the big dogs away."
"They are not very scared then?" said Mum.
"My babies know I will look after them," said Rosie. "I'm their mum."
"How do you look after them?" Mum asked.

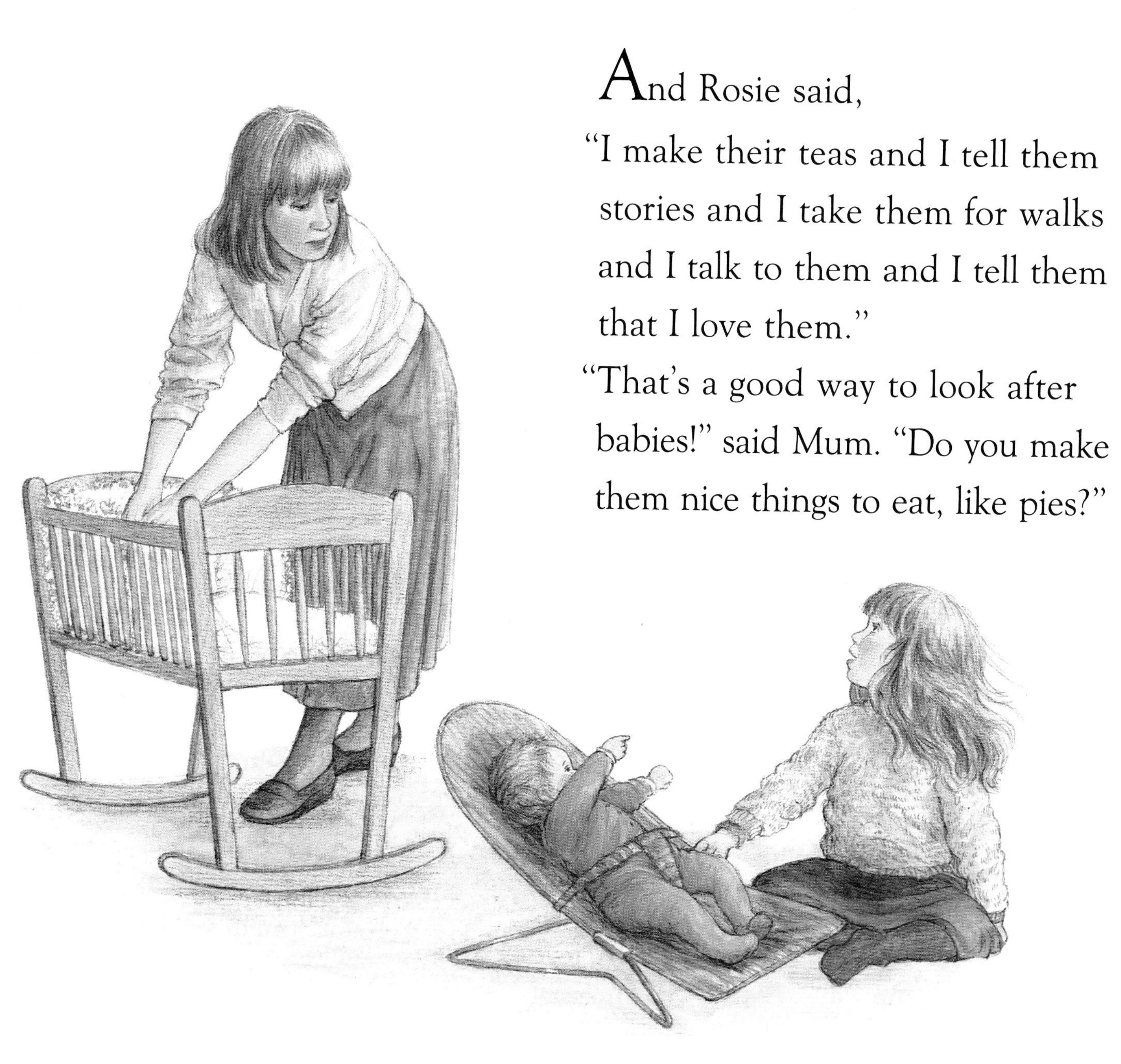

And Rosie said,
"I make their teas and I tell them stories and I take them for walks and I talk to them and I tell them that I love them."
"That's a good way to look after babies!" said Mum. "Do you make them nice things to eat, like pies?"

And Rosie said,
"My babies make their own pies,
but they never eat them."
"What do they eat?" asked Mum.

And Rosie said,
"My babies eat apples and apples and apples all the time. And grapes and pears but they don't like the pips."
"Most babies don't," said Mum.
"Are you going to tell me more about your babies?"

And Rosie thought and thought and thought and then Rosie said, "My babies have gone to bed."

"Just like this one," said Mum.

"I don't want to talk about my babies any more because they are asleep," said Rosie. "I don't want them to wake up, or they'll cry."

"We could talk very softly," said Mum.

"Yes," said Rosie.

"What will we talk about?" asked Mum.

And Rosie said,

"ME!"